Tech-Savvy Parenting

Tech-Savvy Parenting

How to Foster Healthy Screen Habits in Kids and Teens

(A Unique and Practical Guide to Raising Digitally Balanced Children)

Sofia Albrecht

Mindful Pages

Published in 2025

ISBN: 9789371342452 (PB)
ISBN: 9789371348959 (eBook)

Published by

Mindful Pages
Imprint of Alpha Editions LLC
312 W. 2nd St #1834
Casper, WY 82601, USA

This book was developed using advanced writing tools to support the drafting and ideation process. All content has been thoughtfully curated, refined, and reviewed to ensure quality and relevance.

Content

Introduction

The question of how to parent in the digital era is no longer some abstract puzzle for future generations to solve—it's here, pressing into the everyday lives of today's parents, teachers, and caregivers. Screens aren't fixed to the family room television anymore; they're nestled in our children's pockets, strapped to their wrists, flickering quietly on nightstands. They go with them to school, to the dinner table, even to bed. Technology isn't simply present; it's entrenched—shaping not only how children learn, play, and socialise, but how they interpret the world and, crucially, how they come to understand themselves. For those trying to raise children who are not only capable but emotionally attuned and resilient, it can feel like navigating a constantly shifting terrain—guiding a vessel through waters that redraw themselves beneath the keel with each passing moment.

And yet, amid the cacophony of advice about screen time, consensus remains elusive. The debates echo through classrooms, parenting blogs, and family dinners alike: How much is too much? Are all forms of digital engagement created equal? Should we restrict screens altogether, welcome them wholeheartedly, or attempt to strike that ever-elusive balance? Unfortunately, public discourse often collapses into stark binaries: technology is either saviour or scourge; children are enlightened digital natives or hopelessly hooked; parents are permissive or authoritarian. Such rigid thinking obscures a more intricate reality—one this book sets out to uncover.

Tech-Savvy Parenting: How to Foster Healthy Screen Habits in Kids and Teens urges parents to move beyond oversimplified arguments and into a richer, more psychologically grounded conversation. This isn't a manual of hard rules. Nor is it an alarmist tract aimed at provoking guilt or panic. Rather, it's a comprehensive guide, rooted in current neuroscience, developmental psychology, behavioural science, and the lived experience of modern parenting. Its aim isn't to provide quick fixes for "managing" screen time, but to offer parents the tools to understand what's really going on beneath the surface—why screens are so magnetic, how they interact with young minds and emotions, and how we might raise children who are thoughtful, confident, and digitally fluent in a world that won't be unplugging any time soon.

We start by unpicking one of the most persistent fallacies in contemporary parenting: the fixation on screen time as the gold standard of digital health. Chapter One, *The Digital Dilemma – Beyond the Screen Time Debate*, challenges this narrow view, urging a shift away from stopwatch metrics and toward a deeper inquiry into the quality and psychological substance of screen experiences. It's not simply about how many hours a child spends online, but *how* those hours are structured—and, perhaps more crucially, what those digital engagements are displacing. Three hours spent building an app or composing music online is not the same as three hours lost to an endless scroll of algorithm-fed distraction. To guide children wisely, we need to understand the design of the digital environments they inhabit—environments meticulously crafted to capture attention and monetise it, often at the expense of mental clarity and autonomy.

Hence, we delve deeper. Chapter Two, *How Screens Shape the Developing Brain*, explores the neurobiological blueprint of young minds in the midst of digital immersion. The child's brain is exquisitely plastic—malleable, sensitive, and profoundly shaped by repeated interaction. How children use technology can either enhance neural pathways that support innovation, analysis, and resilience, or it can subtly undermine the mental muscles needed for deep focus, emotional regulation, and long-term thinking. By understanding the neurological toll of overstimulation, chronic multitasking, and hyper-speed content shifts, parents can better support the cultivation of not just digital discipline, but what might be called inner ballast—a steadiness of mind and spirit amid digital noise.

But understanding the brain's wiring is only one side of the coin. To meaningfully influence screen habits, one must also reckon with the machinery behind the screens themselves. Chapter Three, *The Science of Persuasive Technology – Who's Really in Control?*, pulls back the curtain on the attention economy. Here we explore how apps, games, and platforms are not benign tools but strategically engineered systems designed to prey on cognitive weak points. Infinite scroll, autoplay, algorithmic feeds—these aren't conveniences; they're behavioural levers. And while they affect all of us, they strike especially hard in the developing minds of children and teenagers. This chapter offers parents a critical toolkit to recognise and resist these design traps—not through blanket restrictions, but by fostering awareness and building intentional, thoughtful use.

Following this, we turn toward what really builds strength: resilience. Chapter Four, *Raising Digitally Resilient Kids*, outlines a framework for fostering self-regulation, emotional intelligence, and wise decision-making in the digital realm. This is not about setting up digital firewalls or laying down curfews like some digital-era tyrant. It's about co-regulating with children, engaging in open dialogue, and crafting boundaries that are responsive rather than rigid. Kids are not just passive recipients of tech—they're agents. They must learn to make discerning choices, and that begins with adults modelling thoughtful behaviour themselves. Resilience, after all, doesn't mean insulating children from every discomfort. It means helping them develop the capacity to face digital difficulties—and recover.

The challenges of digital life are increasingly social and psychological. Chapter Five, *The Social and Emotional Impact of Screen Culture*, examines the fraught world of social media and digital interaction. For today's youth, peer validation is often measured in digital applause—likes, shares, reactions. Social platforms promise connection, yet frequently sow disconnection, anxiety, and distorted self-image. Adolescents navigate a minefield of comparison, curated identities, and cyberbullying that many adults fail to see, let alone understand. This chapter explores how to help children stay grounded in self-worth, teaching them to participate in digital spaces without becoming subsumed by them.

And when tech use begins to spill into every crevice of life—displacing sleep, physical activity, or emotional presence—the conversation takes a more serious turn. Chapter Six, *When Technology Becomes a Problem – Recognising Digital Dependency*, confronts the uncomfortable reality of digital overuse and its kinship with addictive behaviours. Drawing on clinical psychology and behavioural research, this section reframes so-called "screen addiction" not as individual failing, but as a cultural and systemic imbalance—often exacerbated by adult habits that subtly endorse constant connectivity. Here, the book offers tools to assess problematic use, not from a punitive stance, but through honest appraisal and compassionate recalibration.

Yet it would be a mistake to view technology solely through a critical lens. Chapter Seven, *Tech as a Tool for Growth and Creativity*, offers a more expansive vision—one in which technology becomes a platform for ingenuity, not inertia. All screen time is not created equal. When children engage with digital tools to invent, to design, to communicate with intention, they're not being numbed by screens; they're being empowered. From digital storytelling to coding and civic tech projects, today's youth can use digital platforms to build, to learn, and even to lead. Parents are encouraged here not to merely restrict, but to redirect—toward constructive, meaningful engagement.

Finally, Chapter Eight, *A Balanced Approach to Parenting in the Digital Age*, distils the heart of this book's ethos: digital parenting works best when approached as a partnership, not a power struggle. Authoritarian edicts rarely yield lasting results. But when families sit down together to talk values, co-create boundaries, and remain flexible to shifting digital realities, they foster not only responsible habits but deep trust and shared purpose. This final chapter also casts an eye toward the horizon—toward AI, virtual reality, brain-computer interfaces—all of which are fast becoming part of our children's normal. Preparing them for that future means raising not just users, but reflective, ethical participants in the digital age.

What sets this book apart is its refusal to flatten complexity into catchphrases or false choices. Parenting in a digital world demands nuance, vigilance, and a measure of humility. It asks us not only to keep pace with technological change, but to interrogate our own habits and assumptions. What are we modelling? What messages are we sending, inadvertently or not, about attention, presence, value?

Throughout these pages, you'll find rigorous research, yes—but also lived wisdom, case studies, practical frameworks, and hands-on exercises to bring theory into action. There is no single formula here, no master key. Instead, you are invited to craft an approach to digital parenting that reflects your values, your child's needs, and the ever-evolving technological landscape.

Ultimately, *Tech-Savvy Parenting* is about more than helping children "cope" with technology. It's about helping them thrive—thoughtfully, creatively, ethically—in a world that is, like it or not, increasingly digital. Not as enforcers, but as mentors. Not gatekeepers, but fellow travellers.

Chapter 1
The Digital Dilemma – Beyond the Screen Time Debate

There was a time—not so long ago, really—when parental worries about technology were confined to the television perched in the living room corner or the family desktop humming away in a separate study. These devices had boundaries, both physical and temporal. They stayed put, they could be turned off, and they competed—often unsuccessfully—with dinner, conversation, or outdoor play. Fast-forward just a decade or two, and the scene has shifted dramatically. Today's child walks about with a device in their pocket that dwarfs the computing power of the systems that once took astronauts to the moon. And yet, curiously, the public discourse hasn't evolved in step. Parents still ask, often anxiously: *How much screen time is too much?* It's a fair question—but increasingly, it's also the wrong one.

This chapter opens with a challenge to that very premise: that screen time can be sorted into tidy categories of good or bad, safe or dangerous. Life, of course, rarely works that way. And neither does digital engagement. Watching a nature documentary, FaceTiming with a cousin, diving into a complex strategy game, or scrolling through a hyper-edited feed of influencer content—these activities may all involve screens, but the psychological terrain they traverse is wildly different. So the real question isn't simply how *long* children spend in front of screens. It's what those screens are *doing*—to their attention spans, their emotional lives, their social relationships, and their sense of self.

To understand that, we need to peer into the machinery of the mind. At the heart of our response to digital engagement is the brain's reward system—a tightly woven network governed by dopamine, that slippery little neurotransmitter tied to anticipation, pleasure, and habit formation. Modern digital products are not just optimised for convenience or entertainment; they're architected, quite deliberately, to exploit this neurological loop. Each ping, pop-up, like, or game level serves up a tiny dose of reward. Nothing too dramatic on its own—but in aggregate, over time, they condition children (and adults, let's be honest) to reach again, and again, and again.

This reinforcement doesn't just encourage usage; it rewires expectation. Dopamine isn't so much the feel-good chemical as it is the *want-more* chemical. And it's particularly potent when rewards are unpredictable—think slot machines, or loot boxes, or endless social media feeds. The more erratic the gratification, the stronger the behavioural grip. For children—whose prefrontal cortices, the brain regions tied to judgment and self-control, are still under construction—this creates a particular vulnerability. Screens don't just occupy time; they alter mental architecture. They teach children to crave stimulation, to prize novelty, and to resist stillness—traits that, unsurprisingly, don't bode well for learning, emotional regulation, or real-world resilience.

What we're witnessing is the rise of the attention economy—a sprawling commercial ecosystem built on the capture, retention, and monetisation of human focus. Tech giants aren't merely designing products; they're engineering behaviour. Features like infinite scroll, autoplay, and personalised recommendation engines are not conveniences—they're mechanisms of persuasion. And while these systems are not, in themselves, evil, their logic is rarely aligned with a child's cognitive or emotional development. They seek time-on-platform, not depth of understanding. They measure engagement, not growth.

This is where the old screen-time metrics fall short. Counting hours is a poor proxy for gauging impact. A child coding a game for an hour engages very different mental muscles than one glued to uncurated video clips. More than that, screens now bleed into so many dimensions of life—education, communication, creative expression—that strict time limits often miss the point. It's not the number of hours; it's the *quality*, the *context*, and the *intent* behind the interaction. Does it connect? Inspire? Deplete? Distract? These are harder questions, yes—but far more telling.

Instead of issuing blanket bans or falling back on fear, we need a more discerning approach—one grounded in psychological understanding and a bit of everyday common sense. This means teaching children not just how to *use* technology, but how to notice its effects: physically, emotionally, mentally. Not all screen time is created equal, and not all digital experiences are equal in their impact. Some can be nourishing, expansive, even transformative. Others—well, not so much.

And the dopamine circuitry? It's not inherently harmful. It's part of how we're wired to learn and adapt. But it becomes problematic when exploited repetitively in shallow, compulsive ways. A child who instinctively grabs a phone in moments of boredom or discomfort is not simply passing time—they may be cementing a pattern that becomes neurologically ingrained. Yet, if that same child also enjoys rich offline interactions, active play, meaningful rest, and supportive relationships, the occasional digital escape is far less consequential. Balance, as ever, is the crucial—if elusive—goal.

In practical terms, this means helping children develop metacognitive awareness about their screen use. Ask them (and yourself): *How do you feel after using this app? Are you energised or drained? Connected or hollow? Why did you reach for your phone just now—boredom, curiosity, habit?* These aren't always easy conversations, and they may be met with shrugs or silence at first. But over time, they lay the foundation for healthier digital habits—habits rooted in awareness, not just obedience.

A particularly helpful frame here is the contrast between digital natives and digital immigrants. Children today are immersed from birth in a world of touchscreens and voice assistants. They don't distinguish between online and offline life—it's all just *life*. Meanwhile, many of their parents view technology through a more sceptical lens, shaped by a world that once functioned without it. This generational divide, while understandable, can lead to unnecessary friction. Children may see their digital spaces as social and creative; parents may view the same spaces as isolating or superficial. Bridging this gap requires empathy, not just authority. It means stepping into your child's world—not to monitor, but to understand.

One family's experience illustrates this point vividly. Two teenagers, both enthusiastic gamers, were constantly clashing with their parents over screen time. The usual cycle—lectures, confiscations, resentment—played out like clockwork. But then something shifted. The family enrolled in a digital literacy course together, learning how algorithms influence content, how persuasive design works, and how their own habits were being shaped. The parents started asking questions rather than issuing ultimatums. The teens, in turn, began thinking more critically about their digital choices. Together, they crafted a family media agreement—not a list of rules, but a living document grounded in shared values. The battles didn't disappear, but they diminished. Screen use became a subject of conversation, not conflict.

And that, really, is the crux of this chapter: the shift from control to collaboration. The digital world is not something we can wall off with timers and tracking apps. Nor should we try. Our role isn't to banish screens, but to build discernment. To help children become reflective, self-aware users of technology—not passive recipients, but active participants in their digital lives.

The chapters ahead will explore this terrain further—from how screens shape the architecture of the developing brain, to how persuasive technologies work beneath the surface, to how families can cultivate digital resilience that endures. But it all starts here, with a willingness to ask better questions. Not, *How many hours is too many?* but rather: *What's happening to my child when they're online? Is this making them stronger, kinder, more curious—or pulling them in the opposite direction?* These are the conversations worth having. They're messier, yes. But they matter.

The Psychology of Digital Engagement – How Technology Interacts with the Brain's Reward System, Shaping Attention, Learning, and Emotional Development

Children today are growing up in a digital landscape that is not merely influential—it is immersive, adaptive, and psychologically attuned to their every move. From brightly coloured educational apps to fast-paced video games and endlessly scrolling feeds, digital experiences are designed with precision, shaped not just by technological advances but by a deep understanding of human psychology. Central to this design is the brain's reward system—a complex network of neural structures and biochemical signals that influence attention, motivation, learning, and emotion. Understanding how digital technology interacts with this system is key to navigating its effects on child development.

At the heart of this interaction lies dopamine, a neurotransmitter often (and somewhat inaccurately) referred to as the "pleasure chemical." While dopamine is indeed associated with pleasurable experiences, its more fundamental role lies in motivation and reinforcement. It helps us prioritise tasks, seek rewards, and repeat behaviours that yield positive outcomes. The dopamine system evolved to promote survival, reinforcing actions like eating, exploring, and social bonding. However, modern technologies have learned to co-opt this system with remarkable efficiency.

Consider the act of receiving a notification. A message appears on a child's phone, accompanied by a ping and a vibration. That tiny moment triggers a cascade of dopamine release, encouraging the brain to pay attention and respond. Over time, the brain begins to anticipate this stimulus. This anticipation—rather than the actual message—is what generates the strongest dopaminergic response. The result is a behavioural loop that rewards not just the content, but the habit of checking itself. The more unpredictable the reward, the more reinforcing the behaviour. This is the psychological principle behind "variable reward schedules"—the same mechanism that drives compulsive gambling, and now fuels much of modern app design.

One need only look at popular platforms like TikTok, YouTube, or Instagram to see these principles in action. Children are not just watching videos; they are being guided through an experience engineered to maximise engagement. Content is tailored algorithmically to match their preferences, shorten attention cycles, and increase exposure. The autoplay feature, swipe-to-refresh functionality, and dynamic notifications create an environment of perpetual novelty. These platforms aren't simply offering content—they are triggering and training the brain's reward circuits to crave it.

The effects of this kind of interaction extend beyond fleeting moments of gratification. They fundamentally shape how attention is allocated. Unlike focused tasks that require sustained mental effort—such as reading, solving problems, or deep conversations—digital platforms are designed to capture attention in rapid, fragmented bursts. For children, whose attentional systems are still developing, this fragmented engagement can interfere with the brain's ability to regulate focus. Research has shown that frequent switching between digital tasks, or "media multitasking," is associated with diminished working memory, increased distractibility, and a reduced capacity for sustained concentration. While the brain is remarkably plastic, constantly shifting attention weakens the neural circuits required for deep focus, reinforcing habits of mental skimming over cognitive immersion.

This is not merely a theoretical concern. In classrooms, educators report growing challenges in maintaining students' attention across even brief intervals. Children accustomed to fast-paced digital feedback often struggle to tolerate delayed gratification or tasks that require uninterrupted effort. They become conditioned to expect immediate stimuli and may exhibit signs of restlessness or boredom in slower-paced, analogue environments. This shift in attentional capacity has direct consequences for learning outcomes, as many forms of academic success require the very faculties—sustained attention, delayed reward, cognitive flexibility—that digital environments often bypass.

Yet the relationship between digital engagement and learning is not uniformly negative. When designed thoughtfully, digital platforms can stimulate curiosity, reinforce learning through gamified methods, and provide interactive environments that adapt to a child's skill level. For instance, language-learning apps that offer immediate feedback and scaffolded challenges leverage the reward system constructively. These platforms harness dopamine not merely to entertain, but to reinforce productive habits of repetition and mastery. The key distinction lies in whether digital engagement is *purposeful* and *structured*, or *passive* and *indiscriminate*.

The emotional dimension of digital interaction adds another layer of complexity. Children are not just using technology for entertainment or education—they are using it to socialise, seek validation, and make sense of their identities. Social media platforms, in particular, entwine emotional development with algorithmic reinforcement. When a child posts a photo and receives likes, comments, or shares, these signals are processed by the brain as markers of social acceptance. This triggers dopamine release and reinforces the behaviour. Over time, children may begin to measure their self-worth through digital feedback, becoming dependent on external validation. This phenomenon—often referred to as the "validation loop"—can lead to heightened anxiety, reduced self-esteem, and a distorted sense of self.

A study conducted by the University of California, Los Angeles, using functional MRI scans, found that the brain's reward circuitry was significantly more active when adolescents viewed photos with a high number of likes. The same study revealed that young people were more likely to like photos themselves if they had already been liked by many others, indicating a susceptibility to social conformity. This neurobiological response suggests that social media is not just a platform for expression—it is a powerful influence on emotional development, peer dynamics, and identity formation.

One illustrative case involves a 13-year-old girl named Aanya, who began using social media during the COVID-19 lockdown. Initially, her parents viewed it as a way for her to stay connected with friends. However, over several months, Aanya became increasingly anxious about her online presence—obsessively checking for likes, deleting posts that didn't "perform," and withdrawing from offline activities. Her self-image began to fluctuate with each post's reception. Her parents, concerned but unsure how to respond, eventually consulted a psychologist who helped them understand the neurological underpinnings of this behaviour. With structured boundaries, open conversations about digital validation, and a gradual shift toward offline activities, Aanya was able to re-establish a healthier emotional balance. Her story is not unique, but it highlights how deeply digital engagement can intersect with a child's emotional landscape.

The effects are not limited to social media. Video games—especially those incorporating "level-up" mechanics, loot boxes, and real-time social interaction—are potent drivers of reward-seeking behaviour. These games provide clear goals, immediate feedback, and escalating challenges, all of which align perfectly with the dopamine system's architecture. For many children, gaming is not just a pastime—it becomes a source of mastery, identity, and social belonging. While not inherently harmful, excessive gaming can displace other vital activities such as sleep, exercise, face-to-face interaction, and academic effort. Understanding the psychological draw of gaming allows parents to set boundaries not from a place of fear, but from knowledge and empathy.

This insight leads to a fundamental shift in parenting strategy. Instead of viewing screens as simply good or bad, parents can begin to see digital engagement through the lens of behavioural reinforcement. The goal is not to eliminate screen use, but to create environments where technology supports rather than supplants a child's cognitive and emotional development. This includes setting boundaries around screen use before bedtime to protect sleep hygiene, encouraging creative rather than consumptive use of devices, and fostering discussions about how digital experiences make children *feel*—not just what they are doing online.

A promising approach is to cultivate "meta-cognition" in children—the capacity to reflect on their own thoughts, feelings, and behaviours in relation to technology. For example, after using a particular app or playing a game, a child can be guided to ask: Did that activity make me feel energised or drained? Was I using it to connect, to learn, to relax—or just to avoid something uncomfortable? Such reflective practices strengthen self-awareness and help children internalise the principles of healthy digital engagement rather than rely on imposed limits.

As we consider these complexities, it is important to remember that the brain is not a static organ. It develops in response to its environment. While digital technology can shape neural pathways in ways that hinder attention, learning, and emotion regulation, it can also be used intentionally to reinforce positive habits. The outcome depends not solely on the technology itself, but on how it is integrated into a child's broader ecosystem of relationships, routines, and values.

Parents, therefore, have a critical role—not as digital police, but as co-regulators and role models. By demonstrating mindful screen use, prioritising offline connection, and discussing the *why* behind digital choices, adults can foster a home culture where technology is a tool, not a tyrant. This shift requires patience, consistency, and a willingness to engage with the digital world—not fear it. But the long-term benefits are profound: children who can use technology without being used by it, who can focus deeply, learn adaptively, and feel emotionally secure in both online and offline spaces.

The psychology of digital engagement is not a story of villainy and virtue—it is a story of design, development, and deliberate attention. By understanding the reward systems that drive digital habits, we can equip our children with the awareness and agency to thrive in a world saturated with screens, yet still rich in human potential.

The Myth of "Good" and "Bad" Screen Time – Why Categorising Screen Time as Purely Positive or Negative Is Misleading and What Matters More Than Hours Spent on Devices

For years, much of the discourse around children and digital technology has been dominated by a deceptively simple metric: screen time. Parents, educators, and policymakers have often treated it as a digital equivalent of dietary intake—believing that the fewer the hours, the better the outcome. Guidelines have been published, charts distributed, apps developed to monitor and restrict. And yet, despite the widespread adoption of screen time limits, children's digital habits have grown more complex, not less. What this reveals is a core misunderstanding: the assumption that all screen time is functionally equivalent, that it can be assessed in the same way one might count calories or hours of sleep. In reality, this binary view of "good" versus "bad" screen time has outlived its usefulness and risks obscuring the real questions we should be asking.

At its core, the notion of screen time reduction as an end in itself misunderstands the diversity of digital experiences. A child creating an animated film, coding a game, collaborating on a digital art project, or participating in a science webinar is engaging with screens—but in fundamentally different ways from a child mindlessly swiping through short-form entertainment or compulsively checking social media for validation. Both involve screen-based interaction, but their cognitive, emotional, and developmental implications are vastly different. To conflate them under the same metric is to miss the point entirely.

The idea of separating screen time into "good" and "bad" categories is not only reductive but often misleading. It encourages a surface-level response to a deeper set of issues. Time spent on a device becomes the target of scrutiny, rather than the quality of engagement, the psychological context of use, or the broader developmental environment. This can lead to a false sense of security—parents may feel reassured if their child is "under the limit," even if the content consumed is devoid of educational or emotional value. Conversely, guilt and concern may arise when children exceed recommended limits, even if their activities are constructive, collaborative, or creative.

The evolution of digital technology has rendered these metrics even more obsolete. In the past, screen time was largely passive—television, for instance, offered little interactivity. Today's digital landscape is multifaceted. It includes interactive learning platforms, social communication tools, creative software, real-time multiplayer games, and immersive storytelling experiences. Children are no longer mere consumers of content; they are creators, collaborators, and participants in digital ecosystems that blend education, entertainment, and socialisation. Any attempt to evaluate their screen engagement must reflect this complexity.

A growing body of research supports this more nuanced perspective. A 2020 study published in *Nature Human Behaviour* examined the digital habits of over 35,000 children and adolescents and found no consistent correlation between the amount of screen time and psychological well-being. The researchers concluded that other factors—such as sleep quality, physical activity, and family dynamics—had a stronger influence on mental health than screen use alone. Similarly, the American Academy of Pediatrics, once known for strict screen time limits, has updated its stance to focus more on *how* screens are used rather than *how long* they are used. Their Family Media Plan framework encourages parents to consider the content, context, and role of digital technology in family life, shifting attention away from arbitrary time quotas.

Real-world examples further illustrate the inadequacy of the time-based model. Take the case of twelve-year-old Ravi, a quiet but curious boy with a deep interest in astronomy. During the pandemic lockdown, Ravi spent hours on his tablet—not watching cartoons, but exploring NASA's virtual telescopes, taking part in online stargazing communities, and building digital simulations of planetary orbits. His screen time metrics were high, triggering concern from a well-meaning teacher. But a closer look revealed a child fully immersed in self-directed learning, creatively applying knowledge, and forming a sense of identity around a meaningful interest. Ravi's experience exemplifies what some researchers now refer to as *purposeful screen time*—digital engagement that is aligned with personal growth, curiosity, and positive emotion.

Contrast this with the experience of fourteen-year-old Meera, who uses her phone mainly for social media. While outwardly connected, Meera often finishes her screen sessions feeling depleted and anxious. She checks her notifications compulsively, struggles with comparison to online influencers, and finds it difficult to disengage even when she wants to. Her screen time is technically "within limits," yet it regularly undermines her self-esteem and concentration. In this case, it's not the duration of screen use that is the problem, but the nature of the content and its emotional resonance.

This contrast reveals a fundamental truth: the *meaning* of screen time is shaped by context. What was the child's mood before and after? Were they using technology as a creative tool or an emotional crutch? Were they connecting authentically with others or performing for approval? Were they passively absorbing content or actively engaging with it? These are the questions that matter far more than the clock.

It is also important to consider the developmental stage of the child. Younger children, with limited self-regulation skills, may be more vulnerable to overstimulation and difficulty transitioning away from screens. For them, structure and routine are crucial. Adolescents, on the other hand, are navigating identity formation, social comparison, and emotional volatility—all of which can be amplified by digital environments. Their screen use may be more autonomous, but no less in need of guided reflection. A "one-size-fits-all" approach fails to account for these nuances and risks overlooking the very different ways in which children experience digital life.

So how should parents and educators think about screen engagement if the old models no longer apply? A more constructive approach begins by reframing digital use as part of a broader lifestyle ecosystem. Screen time should be evaluated alongside other key developmental needs: sleep, nutrition, physical activity, family interaction, creative expression, and unstructured play. A child whose digital habits support rather than replace these areas is far less likely to experience negative outcomes. The issue is not necessarily screens *versus* real life—it is whether screens are being used in a way that *supports* real life.

This perspective opens the door to more meaningful conversations between parents and children. Rather than enforcing rigid limits, families can begin to co-create media habits based on shared values and mutual understanding. Questions like, "What do you enjoy most about this app?" or "How do you feel after you've been online?" can deepen awareness and prompt children to reflect on their own behaviours. These conversations promote digital literacy, emotional intelligence, and self-regulation—skills that will serve them far beyond the confines of childhood.

It also invites a more collaborative parenting posture. Children are not digital natives simply by virtue of birth; they still need guidance, boundaries, and modelling. Parents can support healthy screen habits by demonstrating mindful use themselves—resisting the urge to multitask constantly, protecting family time from device intrusion, and showing how technology can be used for learning, connection, and creation. When children see adults wrestling with the same questions and making intentional choices, they are more likely to internalise those behaviours.

There is a temptation, particularly when faced with the dizzying pace of technological change, to revert to rigid control or blanket condemnation. But the most effective digital parenting is not reactive—it is reflective. It is less about shielding children from technology and more about preparing them to use it wisely. This requires discernment, dialogue, and a willingness to look beyond the numbers.

The myth of "good" and "bad" screen time is a legacy of a simpler age—one where digital experiences were less varied, less personalised, and less integrated into daily life. Today, we need a new framework—one that recognises the diversity of screen-based activities, the individuality of each child, and the profound influence of context. We need to ask not only *how much* screen time is happening, but *why*, *how*, and *to what effect.*

In embracing this complexity, we do not lose control—we gain clarity. By moving beyond time limits and engaging with the *quality* of screen engagement, we can support children in developing healthy, balanced, and purposeful relationships with technology. Relationships not governed by guilt or anxiety, but by agency, curiosity, and thoughtful participation in a digital world that will be, for them, as real and significant as any offline domain.

The Attention Economy and Your Child – How Tech Companies Engineer Apps and Games to Keep Kids Hooked, and What Parents Need to Know About Persuasive Technology

Attention has become the most valuable commodity in the digital age. No longer merely a cognitive function, it is now currency—measured, bought, and sold with clinical precision. At the heart of today's most successful technologies lies a deliberate and highly sophisticated strategy to capture and monetise human focus. Children, with their developing brains, natural curiosity, and still-maturing capacity for self-regulation, have become a prime target in what has been termed the *attention economy*. For parents seeking to understand why their child struggles to put down a device, resists screen limits, or becomes emotionally dysregulated after extended digital use, the answer lies not in weakness or defiance, but in an invisible war for their child's attention—one that is carefully orchestrated by persuasive technologies.

Persuasive technology refers to digital systems deliberately designed to influence user behaviour. Unlike traditional tools, which operate under user command, persuasive technologies anticipate, nudge, and shape behaviour in real time, often without the user's conscious awareness. The goal is not to offer a neutral platform, but to extend engagement—to keep eyes on screens and fingers tapping for as long as possible. Social media platforms, mobile games, video apps, and even educational tools are now embedded with behavioural design features derived from fields like cognitive psychology, behavioural economics, and neuroscience.

To understand this, we must first acknowledge the key shift in business models. Most digital platforms—especially those available for free—do not sell products. They sell users. More precisely, they sell *access* to users' attention to advertisers and third-party data brokers. In this economy, the longer a person stays on a platform, the more data they generate, the more ads they are exposed to, and the more revenue the platform earns. This model, while lucrative for developers and tech giants, sets up an inherent conflict between user well-being and platform profitability. And when the users are children, the ethical stakes become significantly higher.

A core tactic in this design arsenal is the use of *intermittent variable rewards*—a principle drawn directly from behavioural psychology. Originating from experiments with rats in Skinner boxes, this concept shows that unpredictable rewards are far more effective in reinforcing behaviour than consistent ones. This principle has been digitally repurposed in features like loot boxes in games, "likes" and comments on social media, and algorithmically-generated content feeds that change with every refresh. Each time a child swipes down on a feed or opens a game chest, they are engaging in a behaviour almost indistinguishable from a slot machine pull—an action rewarded sporadically, keeping them hooked through uncertainty.

Another potent design feature is *infinite scroll*, which removes natural stopping cues that might encourage users to take a break. Where a book or a traditional television programme offers natural endpoints, platforms like TikTok, Instagram, and YouTube replace these with an endless stream of content tailored to individual preferences. The lack of friction in these interfaces, paired with machine learning algorithms that adapt to a child's viewing habits, creates an environment optimised not for exploration or learning, but for unbroken immersion.

To see the real-world implications of these features, consider the case of Aryan, a nine-year-old boy who began playing a mobile strategy game that offered "daily login bonuses," limited-time challenges, and ranked competitions. Initially, the game seemed harmless—an engaging blend of puzzles and cartoon battles. Over time, however, Aryan began to exhibit growing anxiety around missing a reward window. He started setting alarms to ensure he didn't miss "event timers" and frequently prioritised the game over meals and playdates. His parents, initially pleased that the game appeared intellectually stimulating, soon realised that his behaviour mirrored addictive patterns. What they hadn't recognised was that the game was deliberately engineered to create compulsive loops—ones that override intrinsic motivation with extrinsic digital incentives.

Another example can be drawn from the way YouTube's recommendation algorithm functions. A study conducted by the Mozilla Foundation found that over 70% of the videos users watched came from algorithmic recommendations, not from intentional searches. For children, this means that a single click on a seemingly benign video can lead to a sequence of increasingly extreme or inappropriate content—driven not by curiosity, but by an AI optimised to increase "watch time." Children are not navigating the internet; they are being led through it by a system that learns from their every interaction, responding not with wisdom or ethics, but with profit-seeking calculation.

Parents often report a sense of helplessness in the face of this invisible architecture. Traditional discipline strategies, such as screen limits or device confiscation, may address the symptoms but do little to illuminate the cause. The deeper issue is not just *what* children are doing online, but *how* their digital environments are constructed to bypass their self-regulatory defences. Understanding this gives parents a strategic advantage—not to fight a losing battle against screens, but to support their children in navigating these systems with informed awareness.

One practical step is to begin discussing persuasive design with children in an age-appropriate way. Just as we teach children to recognise advertising tricks on television or junk food marketing in supermarkets, we can begin to decode digital environments with them. Ask questions like: "Why do you think this app sends you notifications every few hours?" or "How do you feel after using this app for a while?" These conversations foster critical thinking and help children begin to see themselves not just as users, but as *participants* in systems designed to influence them.

Schools and educators also have a role to play. Media literacy curricula that include modules on persuasive technology can empower students to evaluate platforms not just based on content, but on intent. Some forward-thinking educational initiatives are already introducing children to the concept of *attention as a finite resource*—helping them understand that their focus is being solicited by forces outside their control, and that reclaiming it is an act of self-respect.

It's equally important to recognise that not all persuasive design is nefarious. Behavioural science can be used to encourage positive outcomes. Educational platforms that reward consistent effort, mindfulness apps that reinforce healthy habits, and goal-setting tools that use gamification ethically can all support child development. The key difference lies in *intent.* Is the platform designed to help the child grow, reflect, or connect? Or is it designed to extract their attention and data for commercial gain?

An instructive comparison is the contrast between a learning app like Khan Academy and a typical free-to-play mobile game. The former uses engagement loops to encourage mastery and progress—rewarding persistence, offering helpful nudges, and pausing after key learning moments. The latter, more often than not, relies on urgency, scarcity, and distraction. Understanding this distinction enables parents to make more informed decisions about what technologies they allow into their home—and how they talk about them with their children.

At a policy level, growing awareness of the attention economy has sparked international conversations around ethical tech development. Some jurisdictions are exploring regulations on addictive design, particularly for products targeted at minors. There is increasing recognition that children deserve special protections—not just from inappropriate content, but from design practices that exploit cognitive immaturity. While legislation is still evolving, this growing movement signals a shift in public consciousness: a move away from blaming individuals for "overuse," and toward holding systems accountable for their manipulative architecture.

Ultimately, the most powerful antidote to the attention economy is human connection. Children who feel seen, heard, and supported offline are less vulnerable to the siren call of digital validation. Families who prioritise shared meals, outdoor activity, creative pursuits, and face-to-face conversations are building the very skills that persuasive technology seeks to erode—self-awareness, patience, and emotional regulation. These practices may not offer instant results, but they lay the groundwork for digital resilience that will endure.

To raise children in a digital world without falling prey to its traps, we must first name the forces at play. The attention economy is not some abstract threat—it is a meticulously engineered system that thrives on distraction and dependency. But with knowledge, intention, and compassionate guidance, we can help children understand that their attention is not a weakness to be exploited, but a gift to be guarded. And in doing so, we reclaim not only their focus—but their agency, creativity, and capacity for deep, meaningful engagement in both digital and real worlds.

The Role of Dopamine and Digital Habits – An Exploration of the Science Behind Digital Cravings and How Parents Can Help Children Build Healthier Habits

Understanding why digital technologies hold such a powerful grip on children's attention and behaviour requires us to look beyond the surface of entertainment or social connectivity. At the heart of this phenomenon lies a neurochemical process that has evolved to help humans survive but is now being harnessed—some would argue hijacked—by the architecture of modern digital experiences. This process revolves around dopamine, a neurotransmitter often misunderstood in popular discourse as simply the "pleasure chemical." In reality, dopamine is far more nuanced. It governs anticipation, motivation, reward-seeking, and reinforcement—functions essential for learning, memory, and goal-directed behaviour. It is also central to the formation of habits, including those that emerge around technology use.

When a child taps on a video, levels up in a game, or receives a notification on social media, dopamine is released in the brain's reward circuitry. This circuit, which includes regions such as the ventral tegmental area, the nucleus accumbens, and the prefrontal cortex, lights up in response to perceived rewards. But contrary to popular belief, it is not the reward itself that produces the most potent dopamine surge—it is the *anticipation* of it. This explains why children will scroll endlessly through a feed or refresh an app repeatedly: they are not guaranteed satisfaction, but they are primed for the possibility. This kind of variable reinforcement, in which the timing and value of the reward are unpredictable, has been shown to be the most powerful driver of habit formation—a fact that has not escaped the notice of app developers and game designers.

This dynamic was perhaps most famously illustrated in studies of operant conditioning, where animals learned to press levers for food rewards. When rewards were given consistently, the animals' behaviour remained moderate. But when rewards were delivered unpredictably—sometimes after one press, sometimes after five—the response rates skyrocketed. This behavioural model now underpins many digital systems. From loot boxes in video games to autoplay features and algorithmic feeds, platforms are built not just to deliver content, but to exploit the dopamine system's sensitivity to uncertainty and novelty.

The implications for children are particularly significant. During childhood and adolescence, the prefrontal cortex—the brain region responsible for decision-making, impulse control, and long-term planning—is still under development. Meanwhile, the limbic system, including structures that respond to rewards, is highly active. This developmental imbalance means that young users are neurologically predisposed to seek immediate gratification even when it conflicts with longer-term goals. When digital technologies are designed to trigger precisely this mechanism, children are left especially vulnerable to forming compulsive habits.

Consider the example of thirteen-year-old Kavya, who began using a popular short-video app during school holidays. What began as an occasional diversion quickly escalated. She would open the app as soon as she woke up, use it during homework breaks, and spend hours scrolling late into the night. Her parents noticed mood swings, reduced attention during conversations, and persistent sleep problems. When they tried to limit her usage, Kavya became defensive and irritable, insisting she was "just relaxing." What they didn't realise was that her behaviour mirrored a dopamine-driven cycle of habit reinforcement: each short video represented a small potential reward, and the app's algorithm ensured a continuous stream of highly tailored content. Even when the content was mediocre, the intermittent nature of "hits" kept her coming back.

It's important to clarify that dopamine itself is not the villain. It is a crucial neurochemical for healthy development. Children experience dopamine release when learning a new skill, achieving a goal, playing imaginatively, or engaging in meaningful social interactions. In fact, dopamine is essential for motivation and curiosity—qualities that should be cultivated rather than suppressed. The problem arises when digital systems create dopamine loops that bypass meaningful engagement, reinforcing behaviour without deeper cognitive or emotional investment.

The difference between adaptive and maladaptive digital habits often lies in the intention and outcome of the experience. For instance, a child who spends time coding, composing music on a digital platform, or building a virtual world in a game that requires planning and collaboration may also be engaging the dopamine system—but in a way that promotes learning, creativity, and sustained effort. These activities involve intrinsic motivation and tend to offer fewer instant rewards. Conversely, many mainstream apps and games are structured to deliver frequent, low-effort bursts of stimulation—rewards untethered to personal growth or deeper satisfaction.

This distinction points to a vital insight for parents: managing digital habits is not about eliminating all forms of dopamine-triggering activity. It is about redirecting children's natural desire for stimulation and reward toward experiences that build competence, connection, and emotional resilience. Rather than policing screen use through rigid time limits or punitive restrictions, parents can play a more effective role by helping children develop a conscious relationship with their digital environment—one that integrates awareness of how these systems influence behaviour.

One effective strategy is to introduce the concept of *dopamine awareness*. Even young children can begin to understand that their brains respond to patterns, and that not all rewards are equally nourishing. Parents might say, "Have you noticed how hard it is to stop watching after one episode?" or "Why do you think that game makes you want to keep playing even when you're tired?" These reflective questions encourage meta-cognition and begin to build a child's internal compass for assessing digital experiences.

Sleep is a particularly relevant area where dopamine-driven digital habits can wreak havoc. Numerous studies have shown that late-night screen use disrupts circadian rhythms by suppressing melatonin production, especially when exposure to blue light occurs within an hour of bedtime. Beyond the physiological effects, the constant expectation of digital rewards keeps the brain in a heightened state of arousal, making it difficult to wind down. Children who stay up playing games or scrolling through social feeds often report difficulty falling asleep, fragmented rest, and daytime fatigue—all of which impair emotional regulation and academic performance.

This cycle is often unrecognised by both parents and children, who may interpret morning grogginess as laziness or resistance, rather than the downstream effect of a poorly timed dopamine cycle. Addressing this requires more than just earlier bedtimes. It involves creating evening routines that support healthy neurochemistry: dimming lights, turning off screens at least an hour before sleep, and introducing relaxing activities such as reading, conversation, or mindfulness exercises. These practices not only improve rest but also train the brain to decouple reward from screen-based stimulation.

Social media presents its own unique dopamine challenges. Every like, comment, or message delivers a microdose of social validation. Adolescents, whose sense of identity is still forming, are especially susceptible to measuring their self-worth through these metrics. The craving for more likes or the anxiety of comparison can lead to compulsive checking, content performance anxiety, and diminished self-esteem. As one fifteen-year-old girl confided during a digital wellness workshop: "It's not about posting something I like. It's about what I think will get the most attention." Her behaviour reflected a reward system shaped by external metrics rather than internal satisfaction.

Parents can help by fostering discussions around authenticity and value. Asking questions such as "What kind of posts make you feel good for longer?" or "Do you feel better or worse after being on this app?" can create openings for children to evaluate not just how often they use a platform, but why they use it and how it makes them feel. Encouraging children to take breaks from social media and observe how they feel without the constant feedback loop can also re-centre their emotional equilibrium and recalibrate their dopamine responses.

Importantly, children are not passive in this process. They can be empowered to shape their own digital habits when given the tools, language, and support to do so. This may involve co-creating digital boundaries, experimenting with screen-free times during the day, or identifying apps that leave them feeling energised rather than depleted. When children are involved in designing their own digital hygiene, they are far more likely to internalise and sustain those behaviours.

The broader lesson here is that dopamine is neither good nor bad. It is a signal—one that can be used to reinforce both nourishing and harmful patterns. The question is not whether children will seek reward, but what kinds of rewards they are taught to value. Technology is not going away. Nor should it. But it must be integrated into children's lives in ways that respect their neurological development, honour their capacity for deep focus and creativity, and help them build habits that reflect their best selves.

The science of dopamine does not absolve us from responsibility—it clarifies where that responsibility lies. Parents, educators, designers, and policy-makers must work together to ensure that the digital environments children inhabit support, rather than sabotage, their development. By understanding how dopamine shapes digital cravings, and by taking deliberate, compassionate steps to reorient these patterns, we give our children the best chance to thrive not just as consumers of technology, but as conscious participants in the shaping of their own minds.

Case Study: Digital Native vs. Digital Immigrant Parenting – Insights from Real Families Navigating Different Approaches to Screen Time and Digital Engagement

The divide between digital natives and digital immigrants is not just a generational curiosity—it is a lived experience with profound implications for parenting in the modern world. While today's children and teenagers navigate technology as an embedded part of their daily reality, their parents often approach the digital landscape with the memory of a time when screens were optional, episodic, and largely stationary. This divergence creates a unique tension: parents are expected to guide their children through a world they themselves are still learning to understand. As a result, family dynamics around screen time and digital engagement are shaped as much by differing worldviews as by the technologies themselves.

To make sense of this divide, it is useful to understand the core distinction. A *digital native* is someone who has grown up with technology as a natural part of life. From infancy, they've had access to touchscreens, Wi-Fi, streaming platforms, and social media. Their understanding of the digital world is intuitive, fluid, and often emotionally integrated. In contrast, *digital immigrants*—often the parents and educators—came of age in a pre-digital world and have had to adapt. Their understanding of technology tends to be more segmented and analytical, often grounded in caution or unfamiliarity. This difference is not about intelligence or capability—it is about orientation and context.

To explore how these distinctions play out in real families, consider the case of Rohan and Priya, parents of two teenagers in Mumbai. Both professionals in their forties, they are highly educated and digitally literate, yet their relationship with technology is largely functional. They use it for work, communication, and occasional entertainment. Their chil'dren, on the other hand—Anya (15) and Kunal (13)—use digital tools as extensions of identity, creativity, and social belonging. The children move between school assignments, YouTube content creation, gaming, and WhatsApp groups with seamless fluidity. Rohan and Priya, while not resistant to technology, find themselves baffled by the intensity and frequency of their children's screen engagement.

Concerned by what they perceived as "excessive screen time," the parents introduced strict weekday bans on non-academic screen use. This approach, though well-intentioned, created friction. The children felt misunderstood, while the parents felt disrespected. "It's like they don't even see what we do online," Anya explained during a family counselling session. "They think we're wasting time, but they don't understand that this is how we learn, how we connect." The family's challenge was not technological—it was generational. The children were speaking a digital language that their parents had not yet learned to translate.

What helped the family shift was not more rules, but more *curiosity*. Priya began asking Anya about her video editing projects, while Rohan watched Kunal play an online game, asking questions about strategy and social interaction. Slowly, the dynamic changed. The children became more receptive to guidance because they felt seen, and the parents became more effective mentors because they began from a place of engagement rather than judgement. This approach, grounded in empathy and mutual respect, exemplifies a key principle of successful digital parenting: relationship precedes regulation.

In contrast, another family, the Fernandes household in Bangalore, took a different route. Joseph and Maria, both teachers in their fifties, approached technology with deep scepticism. Their teenage son, David, was allowed limited access to devices, with a strong emphasis on offline hobbies, physical play, and academic excellence. "Screens are a distraction," Joseph asserted. "They make children lazy and addicted." This model, while protective, operated from a deficit lens—assuming that screens were inherently harmful unless carefully contained.

For a while, this approach seemed effective. David was focused, disciplined, and academically successful. But during the COVID-19 lockdown, when schooling moved online and peer interaction became digital by necessity, David began to struggle. He lacked the digital fluency to manage online assignments, collaborate on group projects, or socialise with friends in virtual spaces. His sense of isolation grew, and his academic performance declined—not due to screen overuse, but due to underexposure. The family's rigid framework had shielded him from risks, but also from opportunities to build digital confidence and resilience.

This case highlights a different insight: digital avoidance is not a long-term strategy. In a world where digital engagement is increasingly integrated into every aspect of life—from learning and work to social connection and civic participation—children must learn to *navigate* technology, not merely resist it. This does not mean abandoning boundaries, but recalibrating them to reflect both the benefits and the challenges of digital tools.

A third case, that of the Khanna family in Delhi, provides a compelling hybrid approach. Neha and Arvind, in their late thirties, are professionals in the media industry and consider themselves "tech-savvy." Their daughter, Ria, aged eleven, began showing signs of anxiety after joining a popular social media platform used by her peers. Rather than banning the app outright, the Khannas decided to co-use it. They created their own accounts, followed the same creators, and initiated conversations with Ria about trends, messages, and online behaviour. This created an open channel for discussing digital values—privacy, kindness, content curation—without resorting to surveillance or prohibition.

By becoming participants in their daughter's digital life, Neha and Arvind demonstrated that parental involvement need not be oppositional. It can be collaborative, supportive, and informed. This model of *co-engagement* aligns with emerging research showing that children benefit most when adults are involved in their digital lives—not just as gatekeepers, but as guides. According to a study published in the *Journal of Adolescent Health*, adolescents who reported shared media experiences with parents exhibited higher emotional resilience and better online decision-making skills than peers who faced either unregulated freedom or top-down control.

These case studies reveal a broader theme: there is no singular "correct" approach to digital parenting, but there are principles that transcend style. One such principle is *relational attunement*—the capacity to meet children where they are, to listen before advising, and to validate before correcting. Whether a parent is a digital native or a digital immigrant, the foundation of influence is trust. Children are more likely to open up about their digital experiences, risks, and dilemmas when they feel that their perspectives are respected and understood.

This attunement also allows for flexibility in boundaries. Instead of rigid time limits, families might agree on *purpose-based use*—clarifying when screens are for learning, creating, connecting, or relaxing. Instead of defaulting to bans, parents might use *tech breaks* to evaluate digital patterns—choosing days or periods to reflect on habits and recalibrate as needed. These practices are not about relinquishing authority but about strengthening alignment between values and behaviour.

The digital native/digital immigrant divide will not disappear—but it can be bridged. The key is to move from a paradigm of control to one of collaboration. Parents must shift from being distant overseers to engaged mentors, and children must learn to see adults not as digital antagonists, but as allies in navigating complexity. This shift is not always easy. It requires humility from parents and patience from children. But it is possible—and increasingly essential.

As technology continues to evolve, so too must our models of parenting. Artificial intelligence, virtual reality, and immersive learning platforms are already reshaping how children interact with the world. The skills they need—critical thinking, emotional regulation, ethical discernment—will not emerge from digital abstinence alone. They will emerge from lived experience, guided by adults who are willing to step into the digital arena, learn alongside their children, and lead with curiosity rather than fear.

Ultimately, the most effective digital parenting is not about knowing every app or decoding every platform. It is about being present, adaptable, and values-driven. Whether a parent is a digital native or immigrant matters far less than whether they are willing to engage, evolve, and model the kind of thoughtful, balanced digital citizenship they hope to instil. And that, regardless of generation, is a skill that never goes out of date.

Chapter 2
How Screens Shape the Developing Brain

The human brain is far from static; it is a living, changing organism, constantly reshaping itself in response to the world it inhabits. This is especially true during childhood and adolescence—a period of extraordinary neural transformation. Synapses fire and fade, pathways strengthen or wither, and the brain begins to define its own cognitive and emotional contours. These years are not merely a phase of growth; they are the forge in which a child's mental architecture is formed. And in today's world, that forge is increasingly lit by the glow of a screen. To truly grasp what it means to mature in the digital era, we need to peer beyond the interface—deep into the brain's inner workings.

It's no exaggeration to say that digital technology now threads itself through nearly every dimension of childhood development. It shapes how young people learn, how they remember, how they interact with others and navigate emotion. We're long past asking whether screens affect the brain—the real question is when, how, and under what conditions they do. And the answer, frustrating as it may be for those looking for clarity, defies simplicity. The nature of the media, the child's age and temperament, the emotional and social setting—all of these matter. What remains constant, however, is that the brain is sculpted by experience. And digital experiences, in their pace and intensity, are unlike anything the human species evolved to handle.

This is where neural plasticity comes in—the brain's astonishing capacity to rewire itself in response to its environment. It's a gift, certainly, but one that cuts both ways. On the positive side, digital tools can be powerful allies in learning. Interactive media that challenge children to think strategically or solve problems can stimulate the prefrontal cortex. Educational platforms that adjust to a learner's pace may deepen retention and improve cognitive adaptability. And creative software—from animation tools to beginner coding languages—often fosters the kind of planning and abstract thinking that the modern world demands.

But, and it's a significant "but," the same plasticity also leaves the developing brain vulnerable. Constant exposure to fast-moving, low-effort media can condition neural pathways towards distraction rather than focus. The brain, trained to expect instant gratification, becomes restless in the face of slower, more demanding cognitive tasks. Over time, the circuitry reshapes itself—not to reward patience or depth, but to chase novelty. Neuroscientists have a term for this: cognitive fragmentation. It describes a state in which sustained attention becomes harder to achieve, and mental endurance begins to slip.

The evidence is mounting. Brain imaging studies reveal that chronic media multitasking correlates with reduced grey matter in areas responsible for executive control and emotional regulation. Other research links fragmented media use to impaired working memory and a diminished capacity for sustained effort. These aren't just statistical quirks—they signal real, measurable shifts in how young minds are wired to think and feel.

Educators see this firsthand. Increasingly, teachers report that students find it difficult to sink into deep work—those tasks that require extended concentration and internal problem-solving. Instead, many gravitate toward quick fixes: Google searches, chatbots, or digital hints. Helpful as these tools may be in moderation, they can become crutches. When they replace rather than support cognitive effort, the brain begins to lose its grip on persistence, patience, and self-guided learning.

And then there's multitasking—so often touted as a hallmark of digital fluency. Yet research has repeatedly shown that what we call multitasking is really rapid task-switching, and it comes at a cost. Children who believe they're being productive by juggling texts, videos, and assignments are actually paying a hidden toll: slower processing, more mistakes, weaker memory. Over time, this breeds a kind of mental restlessness—a preference for constant motion over thoughtful depth.

Consider the case of Arjun, aged eleven. His parents, concerned about his faltering reading skills and resistance to writing, noticed a pattern. Homework was always accompanied by a swirl of distractions: open tabs, background videos, endless pings. An assessment ruled out any learning disorders, but it highlighted deficits in attention and working memory. Through a deliberate process of reducing screen-related noise and rebuilding focus, Arjun began to recover his ability to engage deeply. His experience is telling—not rare, but representative.

Still, it would be shortsighted to demonise screens altogether. The issue isn't the technology itself, but the quality of engagement it fosters. Passive, disjointed consumption tends to reinforce mental habits that fragment attention. Conversely, digital activities that require reflection, analysis, or creation can strengthen the brain's executive functions. The objective, then, is not abstinence, but curation—steering children toward digital experiences that support rather than undermine their growth.

This becomes even more critical when we consider the world of online information—a world children now inhabit almost as a second nature. It is a chaotic landscape: algorithms dictate visibility, content is designed to provoke, and accuracy often takes a back seat to engagement. In such an environment, the ability to think critically is not a luxury—it's a necessity.

Troublingly, even university students have been shown to struggle with basic media literacy. A study by the Stanford History Education Group found many couldn't distinguish between sponsored posts and reputable journalism, often mistaking superficial polish for trustworthiness. If those at the cusp of adulthood face such challenges, how much harder must it be for children still developing the cognitive tools needed for discernment?

That's why education—at home and in school—must include training in digital scepticism. Children need to be equipped with the habits of mind that question and interrogate, not merely consume. When they come across viral content or emotionally loaded material, they should be encouraged to ask: Who made this? What's their motive? How is my reaction being influenced? These are not innate questions—they must be taught, modelled, practised.

Parents and educators can foster this awareness through something as simple, yet revealing, as an exercise. "A Day in the Digital Life" invites families to reflect together on how they use technology across a typical day. What platforms are used? When? And how do they make each person feel—energised, inspired, disconnected, anxious? The point isn't surveillance or guilt. It's recognition. Awareness, once sparked, has a quiet but transformative power.

Ultimately, the developing brain doesn't just need protection from harmful inputs—it needs nourishment from meaningful ones. As digital media becomes more deeply embedded in children's lives, the task before us shifts. It is no longer about setting limits alone; it is about envisioning what thoughtful, deliberate digital engagement looks like. By tuning into how screens shape the architecture of attention and emotion, and by guiding young people toward habits that strengthen rather than splinter the mind, we can raise a generation capable not just of using technology—but of understanding it, questioning it, and choosing, at times, to turn it off.

The screen, after all, may be a window to the world. But the clarity of what's seen through it depends on the mind that's looking. And that mind, more than any algorithm or app, deserves our fiercest attention.

Neural Plasticity in a Digital World – The Lesser-Known Ways that Interactive Media Strengthens or Weakens Neural Pathways, Influencing Problem-Solving, Memory, and Creativity

The concept of neural plasticity—the brain's extraordinary ability to reorganise itself by forming new neural connections throughout life—has revolutionised our understanding of learning, development, and adaptability. Far from being a fixed structure, the brain is dynamic and malleable, constantly sculpted by experience. For children and adolescents, whose brains are particularly responsive to environmental inputs, this plasticity is both a gift and a vulnerability. In an era where digital technology is ubiquitous, the implications of this adaptability become deeply significant. Interactive media is not merely a passive backdrop to development—it is a powerful shaper of neural architecture, one that can either cultivate or compromise core cognitive functions such as problem-solving, memory, and creativity.

To appreciate the role digital technology plays in shaping the developing brain, we must begin with an understanding of how neural pathways are formed and strengthened. Every experience a child has—every thought repeated, skill practised, or emotion felt—reinforces particular circuits in the brain. The more often a neural pathway is activated, the stronger and more efficient it becomes. This is often summarised by the principle "neurons that fire together, wire together." Conversely, pathways that are underused tend to weaken over time through a process known as synaptic pruning. In the context of screen-based interactions, the question is no longer whether technology affects the brain, but which pathways it is reinforcing—and which it is allowing to wither.

Not all digital interactions are equal in this regard. Interactive media that requires critical engagement, sustained attention, and creative manipulation can stimulate the brain's executive functions and support neurocognitive development. For example, well-designed educational games that challenge users to solve puzzles, plan strategies, or build virtual systems can activate the prefrontal cortex, enhancing cognitive flexibility and decision-making. These activities engage what neuroscientists call "top-down processing," where the brain exerts control over attention and action, enabling deliberate, goal-oriented behaviour.

Take the case of nine-year-old Zoya, an avid user of a digital storytelling platform that allows children to script, animate, and share their own stories. Over the course of a year, Zoya moved from assembling simple image sequences to crafting multi-scene narratives with dialogue, sound effects, and branching storylines. Her teachers noted improvements in her written expression, narrative logic, and visual literacy. In this case, digital engagement was not passive consumption but active construction—an experience that strengthened neural pathways related to sequencing, symbolic reasoning, and working memory.

By contrast, repetitive engagement with fast-paced, low-effort digital content—such as endless scrolling through short-form videos or tapping through idle games—tends to activate more reflexive, bottom-up processing. This style of engagement favours immediate responses over reflective thinking, often bypassing the executive functions that support planning, inhibition, and abstract reasoning. Over time, this can reinforce patterns of fragmented attention and diminished impulse control. These changes may be subtle initially, but their cumulative effect can alter how children learn, remember, and solve problems in broader contexts.

Memory, in particular, is deeply influenced by the quality of engagement. Interactive media can support memory when it requires elaboration, rehearsal, and retrieval practice. Spaced repetition apps for vocabulary building or mathematics, for instance, are based on sound cognitive principles and have been shown to strengthen long-term retention. However, media that delivers rapid, fleeting information without requiring meaningful cognitive engagement can have the opposite effect. Children exposed primarily to such content may develop what researchers term a "transient memory style," where information is quickly absorbed and just as quickly discarded. This undermines the formation of durable memory traces and weakens the neural scaffolding required for complex learning.

Further complicating this landscape is the role of multitasking—a common behaviour among digital natives. Many children toggle between multiple apps, platforms, and notifications while doing homework, attending online classes, or even during meals. Neuroscientific research has consistently shown that the brain is ill-suited to true multitasking. What it actually does is task-switching, which incurs cognitive costs every time attention is shifted. These costs include increased errors, longer task completion times, and impaired memory consolidation. From a neural perspective, constant task-switching leads to the strengthening of pathways associated with distraction and shallow processing, while pathways linked to sustained focus and deep learning are neglected.

This effect is vividly illustrated in the case of Rahul, a fifteen-year-old student who insisted he could study effectively while watching YouTube videos, chatting with friends, and browsing memes. While Rahul could superficially recall facts for quizzes, he struggled with applying concepts in essays or problem-solving tasks. Cognitive assessments revealed a reduced working memory span and impaired attentional control. Once Rahul and his parents introduced structured, distraction-free study sessions—with periods of focused digital engagement interspersed with breaks—his academic performance and self-regulation began to improve. The neural circuits that support executive attention are trainable, but they require intentional practice to thrive.

Creativity, too, is shaped by the type of digital interactions children have. While there is a persistent belief that technology suppresses imagination, the reality is more nuanced. Digital tools can serve as powerful platforms for creative expression—provided they are used as instruments, not ends in themselves. Children who use software to compose music, design games, or create digital art are often engaging in complex forms of symbolic manipulation and iterative thinking. These processes activate brain regions involved in divergent thinking, mental imagery, and conceptual synthesis.

Yet this potential is often unrealised in environments dominated by content consumption rather than creation. Algorithmically curated platforms that serve bite-sized, trending content can crowd out opportunities for imaginative exploration. When every moment of boredom is filled by pre-packaged entertainment, the brain has fewer opportunities to engage in spontaneous ideation or sustained fantasy play—both of which are crucial for the development of creative neural pathways. It is not the screen, but the *structure* of interaction that determines whether neural plasticity is harnessed or hindered.

Given these realities, what can parents and educators do to support healthy brain development in the digital age? The answer lies not in blanket restrictions, but in intentional curation of digital experiences. This includes encouraging activities that require sustained effort, decision-making, and creativity; limiting exposure to low-effort, high-stimulation content; and providing regular opportunities for offline play, social interaction, and unstructured time. These experiences remain irreplaceable in supporting the holistic development of the child's neural, emotional, and social capacities.

One particularly effective strategy is to embed reflection into digital use. After a gaming session or time spent on a creative platform, parents might ask, "What was the most challenging part of that project?" or "How did you solve that problem in the game?" Such questions prompt children to consolidate their learning, reinforcing neural circuits that support meta-cognition and strategic thinking.

The role of sleep also cannot be overstated. Quality rest is essential for synaptic consolidation—the process by which experiences are transformed into long-term neural architecture. Excessive screen use, particularly in the evening hours, disrupts sleep cycles and impairs this process. A simple yet impactful practice is to institute a digital wind-down routine at least an hour before bedtime, replacing screen exposure with calming activities that support neurological recovery and integration.

In classrooms, educators can enhance digital learning by integrating pause-and-reflect strategies, multimodal tasks that combine digital and analogue elements, and collaborative projects that foster both cognitive and interpersonal skill-building. The goal is to create a learning environment where digital tools extend, rather than replace, the brain's natural developmental processes.

Neural plasticity offers both promise and warning. The same mechanisms that allow children to master a musical instrument, learn new languages, or adapt to changing environments can also entrench habits of distraction, shallow thinking, and emotional volatility—depending on how their daily experiences are structured. Interactive media is a potent sculptor of the brain, but it is the quality, context, and intentionality of use that determines the outcome.

We stand at a pivotal moment in child development. The tools our children use today are shaping not only how they think, but *what* they think, and *how well* they can think in the long term. As stewards of their environment—whether as parents, educators, or policymakers—we have a responsibility to ensure that the digital experiences they engage in strengthen the neural foundations for curiosity, resilience, focus, and creativity. It is not enough to ask whether technology is good or bad. We must ask: is it helping our children become the thinkers, learners, and creators they are capable of being? Neural plasticity ensures the brain is always listening. The question is—what are we teaching it to hear?

Cognitive Overload and Shortened Attention Spans – Understanding Why Modern Technology Rewires the Brain for Instant Gratification and What This Means for Learning and Focus

We live in an age where information flows without interruption, alerts ping at every moment, and attention is relentlessly solicited by a multitude of digital devices. For children and adolescents—whose brains are in a state of heightened developmental plasticity—this environment is not simply a backdrop to daily life; it is an active agent in shaping how attention is distributed, processed, and sustained. Among the most pressing concerns for parents, educators, and neuroscientists alike is the phenomenon of cognitive overload and its attendant consequence: the shortening of attention spans. As screens become increasingly embedded in the fabric of childhood, understanding how technology rewires the brain to favour immediacy over depth becomes essential to protecting and nurturing the capacity to learn, reflect, and think critically.

Cognitive overload occurs when the brain is bombarded with more information than it can effectively process, store, or apply. This is not a new concept—humans have always faced limitations in working memory, the mental space used to juggle information in real time. However, the conditions of modern digital life have amplified this challenge exponentially. A child engaging with a single task may simultaneously be processing background music, app notifications, advertisements, and multiple streams of audiovisual input. The working memory, designed for linear, bounded tasks, is now expected to operate in a non-linear, high-frequency landscape with constant switching and sensory stimulation.

The neurological implications of this are considerable. Working memory is governed by regions of the brain such as the dorsolateral prefrontal cortex and the anterior cingulate cortex—both areas still maturing well into late adolescence. When overwhelmed, these systems struggle to filter irrelevant information and maintain sustained focus on a single objective. This leads to fragmented attention, reduced cognitive endurance, and an increased reliance on external cues to guide behaviour. Over time, repeated exposure to high-stimulation environments conditions the brain to prefer novelty, reward immediacy, and resist cognitive effort.

This adaptation is further reinforced by the mechanisms of instant gratification embedded in most digital platforms. Whether it's the swipe of a screen leading to a new video, the rapid levelling-up in a mobile game, or the immediate feedback loop of likes and comments on social media, children are being neurologically trained to expect satisfaction without delay. Dopaminergic pathways associated with reward anticipation become hypersensitised, encouraging behaviours that prioritise short-term rewards over long-term goals. The prefrontal cortex, which is responsible for impulse control and delayed gratification, is effectively sidelined in favour of more reactive, emotionally driven circuits.

Consider the experience of twelve-year-old Leela, who began struggling with reading comprehension and focus in school. Her parents, initially attributing the issue to adolescent restlessness, later realised that her study sessions were punctuated by constant device checking—brief interactions with messaging apps, memes, and video clips. Though individually short, these digital interruptions had a cumulative effect: they disrupted the deep focus required for comprehension and made sustained effort feel laborious and unrewarding. When Leela was guided to implement focused study intervals—using the Pomodoro technique, for instance—and reduce digital interruptions, her academic performance and concentration improved markedly. This change wasn't simply behavioural; it reflected a gradual rewiring of her attentional habits and cognitive stamina.

The shift towards digital multitasking compounds the problem. Children are increasingly expected to juggle multiple inputs—texting while streaming, doing homework while listening to music, and toggling between educational and entertainment tabs. Yet, despite cultural narratives that celebrate multitasking as a modern skill, neuroscience tells a different story. The brain does not perform tasks simultaneously. Instead, it switches between tasks, incurring what are known as "switching costs"—momentary delays, increased error rates, and a weakening of the cognitive residue from previous tasks. These transitions are cognitively expensive and lead to superficial processing.

Research by Clifford Nass and colleagues at Stanford University found that frequent media multitaskers performed worse on measures of task-switching, attention control, and memory retention than those who focused on one task at a time. More disturbingly, the effects were not confined to the moments of multitasking—they appeared to represent a broader cognitive style, one characterised by distraction-seeking and shallow engagement. For children, whose neural networks are still forming the foundations of learning and reasoning, this style can become entrenched, reducing their ability to think deeply, delay gratification, or engage in reflective problem-solving.

Educational environments are not immune to these effects. Classrooms that incorporate digital tools without structured guidance often find students drifting from academic apps to entertainment, even with monitoring software in place. The challenge is not simply access to devices, but the design of those devices to fragment attention. A well-intentioned educational game or video may be hosted on a platform that surrounds it with unrelated advertisements, suggested videos, or autoplay features. The result is a battleground for cognitive resources, with learning competing against an ecosystem optimised for clicks, not comprehension.

It is essential to distinguish between high-quality digital engagement and overstimulation. Tools that encourage deep thinking—such as simulations, creative software, and learning apps that promote spaced repetition and mastery—can support sustained focus and reinforce neural circuits associated with working memory and executive function. The danger arises when these tools are embedded in environments that reward constant novelty. The very structure of platforms like YouTube or TikTok, for instance, discourages long-form engagement. The child who begins watching an educational video may be algorithmically led to progressively shorter, more stimulating, but less cognitively enriching content. This shift is not random—it reflects a design ethos aimed at maximising engagement through speed and sensation.

These patterns extend into the home environment as well. Many families now operate with a "second screen" culture, where television, tablets, and phones are used simultaneously or as background to other activities. While this may appear innocuous, especially during downtime, it subtly trains the brain to expect constant multi-source input. Boredom—once a space for imaginative thinking and introspection—becomes intolerable. Yet boredom is not a flaw; it is a developmental necessity. It creates the psychological space in which children learn to generate their own thoughts, persist in tasks, and access creativity. When every spare moment is filled by a screen, this essential mental space is lost.

Reclaiming focus in a world of instant gratification requires more than curfews or parental controls. It demands a reorientation of values and routines that places depth over immediacy. Parents and educators can begin by modelling focus—demonstrating the discipline of single-tasking, digital-free conversation, and sustained engagement with books, projects, or physical play. Structured digital hygiene routines, such as screen-free zones during meals and before bedtime, help create the mental conditions for consolidation and reflection. Additionally, children benefit from explicit discussions about attention as a skill, not a given. When they understand that their brains can be trained to focus—and that doing so benefits their learning, memory, and sense of agency—they are more likely to take ownership of their habits.

Importantly, interventions must also address the design of digital tools themselves. Ethical technology design, which prioritises well-being over engagement metrics, can reduce cognitive overload by minimising unnecessary alerts, limiting autoplay features, and encouraging breaks. Some platforms are already experimenting with friction—small delays or prompts that make users pause before continuing—so as to encourage more mindful interaction. Supporting such developments and advocating for child-centred design is a critical frontier in digital education.

Ultimately, the challenge of cognitive overload and shortened attention spans is not one of morality, but of development. The digital world is not inherently harmful, but its current design favours the path of least resistance—momentary gratification over enduring growth. For children, whose cognitive capacities are still emerging, this path can divert them from the deeper rewards of learning, reflection, and mastery. The role of adults, therefore, is not to vilify technology but to guide its use, to help children build the mental muscles that allow them to navigate complexity, resist distraction, and remain present with what matters.

If attention is the gateway to learning, then protecting it is not a peripheral concern—it is foundational. In shaping environments that respect the limits of working memory, prioritise meaningful engagement, and resist the lure of constant stimulation, we do more than preserve focus. We preserve the child's capacity for thought itself. And that, in a world saturated with noise, may be the most valuable gift we can offer.

The Dark Side of Multitasking – Debunking the Myth of Productive Digital Multitasking and How Constant Device-Switching Impacts Deep Thinking and Emotional Regulation

Multitasking has become a badge of honour in contemporary culture. The image of a teenager juggling homework, streaming music, answering messages, and browsing social media is often framed as a sign of adaptability, of being a product of the digital age. Parents may marvel—or despair—at their children's apparent ability to handle multiple tasks simultaneously, believing this reflects a new kind of intelligence, one more attuned to the rapid demands of modern life. But neuroscience paints a very different picture. Far from enhancing productivity or cognitive ability, digital multitasking compromises the brain's ability to concentrate, reason deeply, and regulate emotion. The perceived efficiency is, in truth, a costly illusion.

At the core of this misconception lies a fundamental misunderstanding of how the brain operates. Despite popular belief, the human brain cannot perform multiple high-cognition tasks simultaneously. Rather, it shifts attention rapidly between tasks—a process known as task-switching. Each switch, however brief, comes at a cognitive cost. It takes time for the brain to reorient, reprocess, and refocus after each transition. This lag, though seemingly imperceptible, accumulates over time and results in increased errors, reduced memory retention, and diminished performance.

These costs are not abstract. In a widely cited study conducted at Stanford University, researchers Clifford Nass and Eyal Ophir found that individuals who frequently multitasked with digital media were significantly worse at filtering irrelevant information, switching between tasks, and maintaining working memory. What's more revealing is that the more confident individuals were in their ability to multitask, the poorer their actual cognitive performance. In other words, multitasking not only impairs cognitive functioning—it undermines the self-awareness necessary to recognise that impairment.

For children and adolescents, whose brains are still developing the very systems responsible for attention control and executive function, the effects of chronic multitasking are particularly concerning. The prefrontal cortex, which governs self-regulation, planning, and decision-making, continues to mature into early adulthood. When this region is consistently bypassed in favour of reactive, dopamine-driven engagement with multiple devices, its development is disrupted. The brain becomes wired for responsiveness, not reflection—for novelty-seeking rather than sustained engagement.

This neurological shift has profound consequences for deep thinking. Tasks that require extended concentration—such as reading complex texts, solving multi-step problems, or composing thoughtful responses—are particularly vulnerable. These activities rely on the brain's ability to hold information in mind, suppress distractions, and synthesise ideas across time. When attention is continually fractured, the brain struggles to maintain the mental architecture needed for depth. The result is superficial processing, disjointed reasoning, and an increased reliance on external scaffolds—search engines, prompts, and autocomplete functions.

A case study from an urban secondary school in Delhi illustrates this vividly. A group of students, known for their enthusiasm in STEM subjects, began underperforming in problem-solving assessments. Teachers noted that although the students could recall facts and solve routine problems, they struggled with open-ended questions requiring sustained analysis. A classroom observation revealed that many of these students habitually switched between apps while studying—checking messages, browsing YouTube tutorials, and using social media. A pilot intervention that introduced structured, single-task study sessions and digital-free intervals led to measurable improvements in performance within just a few weeks. The change wasn't due to new material or intelligence gains—it was the restoration of uninterrupted cognitive engagement.

Beyond cognition, the effects of digital multitasking also extend into the emotional domain. Emotional regulation depends on the brain's ability to monitor internal states, interpret contextual cues, and adjust responses accordingly. These skills are honed through presence—being attuned to one's thoughts, emotions, and bodily sensations over time. Constant device-switching, however, fragments this self-awareness. Children who are frequently pulled between apps, platforms, and sensory inputs are less likely to notice when they are becoming overwhelmed, anxious, or fatigued. Their internal cues are drowned out by external stimulation.

Research from the University of Michigan has shown that individuals who engage in frequent media multitasking report higher levels of stress and emotional volatility. In children, this often manifests as irritability, impulsivity, and mood swings—behaviours that are sometimes misattributed to temperament or hormones, but are exacerbated by neurological overstimulation. Emotional maturity requires a slowing down of internal processing, a space for feelings to emerge, be named, and be regulated. Multitasking undermines this process by keeping the brain in a perpetual state of partial attention.

This emotional erosion can impact relationships as well. When children divide their attention across devices during conversations, meals, or shared activities, their capacity for empathy diminishes. Empathy, like concentration, is built through presence. It requires attunement to subtle cues—facial expressions, pauses, shifts in tone—that are easily missed when attention is scattered. Over time, this can weaken the bonds of trust and intimacy that are foundational to psychological well-being.

None of this is to suggest that technology, in itself, is harmful. The danger lies not in the presence of devices, but in their design and use patterns. Many apps and platforms are engineered to sustain attention not through depth, but through constant interruption. Notifications, alerts, and auto-play features keep users engaged by triggering the brain's reward circuitry. When children move between these stimuli without pause, they are effectively being trained out of patience and into perpetual reactivity.

The good news is that attention and emotional regulation are skills—skills that can be cultivated, protected, and restored. Families can begin by recognising and naming the myth of multitasking for what it is: a cultural fantasy that masks neurological fragmentation. By modelling single-tasking—reading without checking messages, holding uninterrupted conversations, or watching a film without a second screen—parents can demonstrate that depth has value. Even brief, consistent practices can recalibrate attention. Ten minutes of device-free reading, mindfulness, or focused writing each day can help rebuild the neural pathways associated with concentration and reflection.

Schools, too, have a role to play. Rather than encouraging multitasking as a sign of technological fluency, educators can teach metacognitive strategies that support intentional task management. This includes creating learning environments with clear expectations around focus, embedding reflective pauses into lessons, and encouraging students to notice how they feel and think when they multitask. These habits are not about technophobia—they are about cognitive sustainability in a digital world.

Digital developers must also take responsibility. Just as industries once evolved to consider the public health consequences of their products, the tech industry must design with neurodevelopment in mind. Features that encourage friction—such as prompts that ask, "Are you sure you want to switch tasks?" or limits on simultaneous app use—can nudge users towards more intentional patterns. This is not an affront to innovation; it is an evolution towards ethically responsible design.

Ultimately, the myth of multitasking is not merely a cognitive issue—it is a moral one. When we sell children the idea that they must always be doing more, switching faster, and consuming endlessly, we strip them of the very capacities that make learning, reflection, and empathy possible. By helping them reclaim the ability to do one thing at a time—and do it well—we are not holding them back. We are giving them the tools to go further, think deeper, and feel more fully. In a world obsessed with speed, single-tasking is not a regression. It is a quiet revolution.

Boosting Critical Thinking in a Misinformation Age – How AI-Generated Content, Deepfakes, and Social Media Trends Affect Cognitive Biases and How Kids Can Learn to Discern Truth from Fiction

The 21st-century child is growing up in a world saturated with information—yet not all information is created equal. Between algorithmically curated content, viral misinformation, AI-generated media, and deepfakes that convincingly blur reality and fabrication, the modern digital landscape presents not only a challenge to comprehension, but a fundamental test of discernment. In such an environment, where truth can be manipulated and falsehoods travel faster than facts, the ability to think critically is no longer a luxury reserved for academics—it is an essential survival skill.

At the core of this challenge lies a disjunction between the speed of information dissemination and the pace of cognitive processing. Digital content, particularly on social media platforms, is engineered for maximum engagement, not accuracy. The more sensational or emotionally charged a piece of content, the more likely it is to be shared, clicked, and believed. This dynamic exploits cognitive biases—mental shortcuts the brain uses to simplify decision-making—that can distort judgment and reinforce false beliefs. Confirmation bias, for instance, leads individuals to seek and favour information that aligns with their existing views, while availability bias causes them to overestimate the relevance of information that is most easily recalled, often because it is recent, vivid, or emotionally impactful.

Children and adolescents, still developing the neural circuitry responsible for reflective reasoning and impulse control, are especially vulnerable. The prefrontal cortex—responsible for evaluating evidence, weighing consequences, and resisting emotional reactivity—is not fully matured until the mid-twenties. In the interim, the limbic system, which governs reward-seeking and emotional processing, often dominates. This biological reality means that young people are more susceptible to content that is novel, provocative, or affirming of their social identity, regardless of its truth value.

The rise of AI-generated content complicates this further. Tools that can produce persuasive text, images, audio, and video indistinguishable from human-made content are now widely accessible. While these tools offer remarkable opportunities for creativity and communication, they also erode traditional markers of authenticity. A deepfake video of a political figure saying something inflammatory, a chatbot spreading pseudo-scientific narratives, or a fabricated news headline with AI-generated bylines can all easily bypass a child's still-developing analytical defences. What was once a skill rooted in identifying cues such as tone, visual quality, or linguistic coherence must now evolve into a more nuanced, interrogative mindset.

Consider the case of a classroom project in a high school in Hyderabad where students were asked to research climate change using online sources. One group cited a professional-looking article that denied human influence on global warming. Upon closer examination, the article was traced to a site designed to appear journalistic but funded by fossil fuel interests. Another group quoted statistics from a viral infographic that had circulated on Instagram, unaware that it had been debunked months earlier by scientific organisations. These students were not lacking intelligence—they were lacking tools. Their error was not in trusting information, but in trusting *too quickly*, without critical interrogation.

The challenge, then, is not to teach children what to think, but how to think *about* what they think. This distinction matters. Critical thinking is not simply skepticism or fact-checking—it is the capacity to question assumptions, examine evidence, consider alternative viewpoints, and reach reasoned conclusions. In a misinformation age, cultivating this capacity must begin early and be reinforced often.

One foundational element is helping children recognise their own cognitive biases. This can be done through guided reflection, classroom dialogue, and parent-child discussions. Asking questions like, "Why do you think this post made you feel that way?" or "What do you think the author wants you to believe?" encourages metacognition—the ability to think about one's own thinking. Research from the University of Cambridge's Digital Literacy Project suggests that students who engage in such reflective questioning are more likely to resist manipulative content and to reconsider previously held assumptions when presented with new evidence.

Equally important is the skill of lateral reading—a strategy used by professional fact-checkers that involves leaving a source to verify its credibility through other, independent channels. Unlike vertical reading, which involves scrutinising a single site or document in isolation, lateral reading recognises that truth emerges through comparison, not isolation. Teaching children to open new tabs, cross-reference claims, and check author credentials cultivates habits of mind that slow down reflexive acceptance and foster investigative curiosity.

Yet critical thinking does not emerge in a vacuum. It requires a supportive ecosystem—at home, at school, and online. Parents can play a crucial role by modelling critical engagement themselves. This means being willing to say, "I'm not sure if that's true; let's check," or "That sounds convincing, but who's behind it?" When children see adults grappling with uncertainty and engaging in open-ended inquiry, they internalise the message that critical thinking is a valued, everyday practice—not a chore or a correction.

Educators, likewise, can design curricula that integrate media analysis across subjects. Whether it's evaluating primary sources in history, dissecting arguments in literature, or examining data in science, students should be consistently encouraged to ask: Who made this? Why? What is being left out? How do I know it's credible? Embedding such inquiry-based learning into routine instruction develops not only information literacy but also intellectual humility—a key trait in the resistance to misinformation.

Technological tools can also support this effort. Browser extensions that flag questionable content, platforms that provide contextual information about news sources, and gamified critical thinking apps can all scaffold young users' analytical skills. However, these tools must be used with care. Overreliance can foster complacency, leading children to outsource their judgment to algorithms. The goal should always be to reinforce *human* reasoning, not to replace it.

A particularly powerful approach lies in storytelling. When students hear narratives of individuals who changed their minds based on evidence—whether scientists revising theories, journalists correcting reports, or ordinary citizens challenging misinformation—they learn that intellectual flexibility is not weakness, but strength. These stories humanise the abstract concept of critical thinking, showing that it is both courageous and necessary.

Consider the case of Anaya, a 14-year-old student who was convinced by an online video that certain vaccines were harmful. Rather than confronting her directly, her teacher asked the class to research the history of vaccine development, explore how peer-reviewed studies work, and examine how misinformation spreads. Through this process, Anaya discovered the flaws in her source and arrived at her own revised conclusion. She wasn't humiliated—she was empowered. And perhaps more importantly, she learned that truth is something one must *work* to understand, not something passively consumed.

There are, of course, deeper cultural and emotional factors that make misinformation appealing. Content that confirms identity, alleviates anxiety, or simplifies complexity is often more attractive than nuanced truth. This is why critical thinking education must also address emotional literacy. Helping children recognise when they are feeling fearful, defensive, or overconfident can interrupt the automatic acceptance of comforting falsehoods. Emotional regulation, grounded in self-awareness, enhances cognitive resilience.

Finally, we must resist the temptation to over-simplify the problem. The battle against misinformation is not merely about weeding out falsehoods. It is about cultivating minds that are sceptical without being cynical, open without being naïve, and informed without being rigid. It requires a reorientation of digital life—not as a passive arena of consumption, but as a participatory space for inquiry, reflection, and ethical engagement.

Children will grow up in a world where AI-generated content, deepfakes, and persuasive digital narratives are part of the fabric of daily life. Shielding them entirely is neither possible nor desirable. But preparing them—intellectually, emotionally, and ethically—is both possible and imperative. By teaching them to slow down, question deeply, cross-check widely, and reflect honestly, we equip them not just to survive in a misinformation age, but to thrive within it—as thinkers, as citizens, and as future shapers of a more discerning digital world.

Interactive Exercise: A "Day in the Digital Life" Analysis – A Guided Activity for Parents and Kids to Reflect on How Their Digital Habits Shape Cognitive and Emotional Health

The most profound influences on a child's development are often those that go unnoticed—quietly integrated into daily routines, repeated with little scrutiny, and eventually normalised as harmless or inevitable. Among these, digital habits are perhaps the most pervasive and the least examined. Screens now structure the way children learn, play, communicate, rest, and even regulate emotion. Yet the question of how these interactions shape cognitive and emotional well-being is rarely addressed with the kind of clarity and intentionality it demands. An effective way to bridge this gap is through a guided self-inquiry exercise—a "Day in the Digital Life" analysis—designed not to assign blame or impose restrictions, but to illuminate patterns, promote reflection, and foster a healthier relationship with technology.

At its core, this exercise is a tool for building awareness. Awareness is the first step in behavioural change, especially for habits that operate on autopilot. Children, like adults, often underestimate the amount of time they spend on screens, misjudge the emotional effects of digital engagement, and fail to connect certain cognitive difficulties—like forgetfulness or irritability—to fragmented attention and overstimulation. By co-creating a detailed digital diary and analysing it together, families can bring these invisible dynamics into conscious view.

This process starts by capturing a full 24-hour snapshot of digital interactions. Ideally, this should be done collaboratively, with both the child and parent participating—not just to track usage, but to contextualise it. The goal is not surveillance, but shared inquiry. A parent might begin by noting, "I realised I checked my email six times before breakfast," while a child might observe, "I watched videos during lunch even though I wasn't really paying attention."

These admissions lay the foundation for a non-judgemental conversation, grounded in mutual curiosity.

To bring depth to the reflection, it is important to go beyond measuring screen time in minutes and hours. Instead, each digital interaction should be framed with a few key questions: What was the purpose of the activity—entertainment, socialising, education, distraction? How did I feel before, during, and after? Was this interaction energising, draining, calming, or agitating? What did it replace—a face-to-face interaction, a moment of rest, or a creative task? These questions open a window into the emotional and cognitive footprint of digital habits—insights far more revealing than raw usage data.

Take the example of Aarav, a 13-year-old student whose parents were concerned about his slipping grades and persistent moodiness. Over the course of their digital diary exercise, the family discovered that Aarav spent nearly four hours daily on short-form video platforms—not in one sitting, but in dozens of micro-interactions spread throughout the day. He often turned to his phone during moments of boredom, stress, or fatigue. These sessions left him momentarily distracted but ultimately more anxious, especially before bed. The family hadn't realised that this seemingly harmless habit was interrupting his cognitive rhythm, fragmenting his focus, and overstimulating him before sleep. Importantly, Aarav hadn't realised it either—until he saw it mapped out in front of him.

The exercise also helped Aarav identify activities that supported his well-being. He noted that the days when he spent more time creating digital art or video editing—activities that engaged his attention, creativity, and sense of achievement—he felt more content and focused. These insights didn't come from external rules or parental directives, but from his own observations. Empowered by this self-awareness, Aarav began to restructure his digital habits, not out of obligation but with a clear understanding of what served him and what didn't.

This shift—from imposed control to internalised self-regulation—is critical. One of the greatest challenges in digital parenting is fostering autonomy without enabling overexposure. When children feel controlled, they often resist, conceal, or justify their behaviours. When they are invited into reflective practices, they begin to own their choices. A "Day in the Digital Life" analysis thus becomes a tool not only for behavioural insight but for cultivating meta-cognitive awareness—the ability to think about one's thinking and evaluate one's actions.

Cognitive and emotional health are not abstract states; they are continuously shaped by the micro-choices made throughout the day. Whether to check a notification or stay immersed in a task. Whether to respond to boredom with a scroll or a sketch. Whether to use technology as a crutch or a conduit. Over time, these choices create patterns. And patterns, when repeated often enough, become neural pathways.

Neuroscience underscores this point with growing clarity. Repeated task-switching, common among children juggling apps, platforms, and media streams, weakens working memory and reduces cognitive endurance. Emotional reactivity is heightened by the unpredictability of digital feedback—likes, comments, and messages—that activate the brain's reward system and make it harder to disengage. Sleep quality is degraded not just by late-night use, but by the type of content consumed and the absence of a psychological wind-down. Each of these outcomes is the product of seemingly minor decisions whose cumulative effect is significant.

Through this lens, the "Day in the Digital Life" exercise becomes a diagnostic tool—not in the medical sense, but in the developmental one. It offers a framework for identifying which habits are constructive, which are corrosive, and which are context-dependent. A child who uses screens to decompress after school may benefit from that downtime—unless it bleeds into the hours needed for homework or sleep. A teen who engages in digital activism may be developing valuable civic skills—unless the exposure to polarising content leads to chronic stress. The nuance matters.

For this reason, the reflective analysis should also include a component of goal setting. Once patterns are identified, parents and children can collaboratively establish small, meaningful adjustments. These might include instituting device-free meals, designating screen-free hours before bedtime, or creating "intention statements" before using a device ("I'm watching this to relax for 30 minutes" versus "I'm just checking to see what's new"). The aim is not digital abstinence, but intentionality. To use screens *with purpose* rather than by default.

Importantly, the exercise should also be revisited periodically. Digital habits evolve with developmental stages, academic demands, social changes, and technological trends. What was once manageable may become excessive; what once served a need may begin to displace other vital experiences. By returning to this exercise every few months—or whenever tensions arise around screen use—families can maintain an adaptive, responsive approach to digital engagement.

Beyond individual families, this kind of reflective practice holds promise at the community and institutional level. Schools can incorporate "digital literacy days" where students map their tech use, discuss its effects, and share strategies for healthy balance. Mental health professionals can use the framework in counselling settings to contextualise behavioural symptoms. Even developers and designers, if guided by child-centred insights, could benefit from understanding how their platforms intersect with young users' cognitive and emotional rhythms.

The digital world is not inherently toxic, nor is it uniformly benign. It is a tool—one of extraordinary power—whose impact depends largely on how it is used, and how thoughtfully that use is examined. A "Day in the Digital Life" analysis transforms the act of looking at screens into the act of *looking at oneself*—a mirror not of habits alone, but of needs, desires, vulnerabilities, and values. It asks children not just what they're doing, but who they're becoming through what they do.

For parents and caregivers, it offers a rare opportunity: to step out of the policing role and into the posture of a co-inquirer. To move from "How do I stop this behaviour?" to "What are we learning from this pattern?" To model reflection, invite dialogue, and cultivate the inner compass every child needs to navigate not just the digital world, but the wider landscape of their lives.

When awareness deepens, choices expand. And in that expansion lies the possibility—not of perfection, but of balance, resilience, and a renewed sense of control in a world that often feels as if it's spinning too fast.

Chapter 3
The Science of Persuasive Technology – Who's Really in Control?

At the centre of today's digital conundrum lies a deceptively simple question: who is actually in control? It's not a new question, certainly, but one that has taken on a sharper edge in the age of persuasive technology. When a child swipes through a video feed, taps on a news snippet, or chats with an AI-generated persona, they aren't just consuming. They're entering ecosystems intentionally crafted to influence—to pull, prod, and shape behaviour in ways both subtle and sustained. These are not passive tools. They are, by design, persuasive—created not merely to inform or entertain, but to direct human choices, often without our conscious consent.

This shift in technological design calls for a parallel shift in how we understand digital engagement. Gone are the days when screens could be dismissed as neutral platforms, mere channels for communication. Increasingly, what lies behind them is a blend of behavioural psychology and machine learning, orchestrated to maximise engagement. And what does "engagement" typically mean in these systems? Time spent, emotional intensity, user retention. For children and teenagers—whose brains are still in the slow work of constructing emotional regulation, impulse control, and identity—the implications are particularly stark. These technologies don't just reflect their preferences; they shape them. They reward immediacy, stimulate dopamine systems with perfectly timed feedback loops, and flood their feeds with content so tailored it often knows them better than they know themselves.

Take infinite scroll, for instance. It's become so common we barely register it, but it represents a profound departure from traditional media structure. A book ends, an episode wraps up, a webpage reaches its bottom. But here? There's no end. Just more—always more. Each flick of the finger brings something new, and therein lies the trap. The brain, hardwired to respond to novelty and the lure of unpredictability, finds itself pulled into an experience without boundaries. For a developing mind, still working out how to pause, reflect, and choose consciously, this is particularly hard to resist.

Then come the thumbnails and headlines—the bright lights in this digital arcade. Provocative, sometimes absurd, often manipulative, they promise far more than they deliver. Designed to incite curiosity, outrage, or laughter, they trade on emotion, not depth. Children, who are less attuned to the subtle cues of credibility and intent, often take such content at face value. Over time, this recalibrates their attention. They begin to associate value with immediacy and drama rather than with substance or nuance. What's loud wins. What's quiet—thoughtful, complex, challenging—gets lost in the scroll.

But perhaps the most insidious architect of all is the algorithm. Every major platform runs on it, yet few truly understand how it works. These aren't just mathematical sequences; they're dynamic systems, constantly learning from user behaviour—what you click, pause on, skip, rewatch—and using that data to shape what you'll see next. For children, this creates highly personalised bubbles of content, echo chambers in miniature. What they already like, they'll see more of. What challenges their views or introduces unfamiliar perspectives? That quietly disappears from view.

At first glance, this kind of personalisation might feel like magic. The content seems tailor-made—relevant, entertaining, eerily well-timed. But this apparent relevance often comes at a hidden cost. Children exposed to the same types of content over and over can lose their tolerance for ambiguity or dissent. They start confusing what is popular with what is important, what feels familiar with what is true. And because the algorithm's logic is opaque—even, in some cases, to those who built it—there's little awareness of the process unfolding behind the screen. What emerges is a troubling paradox: children feeling autonomous, while in fact being gently—but firmly—steered.

Understandably, many parents find this daunting. The mechanisms are technical, the behaviours subtle, and the impact slow to reveal itself. But here's the good news: once these systems are named, they can be questioned. And with questioning comes the potential for agency. It begins with conversation—not lectures, but shared inquiry. "Why do you think this video came up next?" "What happens if you stop clicking on that kind of content?" "Who gains when you stay on this app for hours?" These are not rhetorical traps—they are openings for reflection, the first cracks in the wall of digital illusion.

Experiential exercises can help bring this reflection to life. One such example is the "30-Day Algorithm Awareness Experiment"—a simple yet powerful challenge where families agree to disrupt their usual digital habits. They might search topics outside their comfort zones, interact with new creators, or purposely click on content they'd normally ignore. The results are often startling. In one family from Pune, two teenagers watched in real time as their feeds changed—new suggestions, unfamiliar voices, different emotional tones. What began as a game became a wake-up call: their online experiences, they realised, were far from organic.

Another emerging terrain in persuasive tech involves AI-driven companionship—virtual influencers, chatbots, and synthetic "friends" that mimic empathy and responsiveness. These digital personas are often pitched as harmless fun, or even emotional support. But they carry deeper questions. What happens when a child begins to trust, or even confide in, an AI designed not to care but to retain attention? What ethical lines are crossed when a machine mimics intimacy for the sake of engagement?

These are not hypothetical musings; they're real dilemmas families are beginning to face. To navigate them, we must help children distinguish between real connection and algorithmic mimicry. Parents might ask: "Does this chatbot actually understand you—or does it just mirror back what you want to hear?" or "How do you feel after spending time with your AI friend—calmer, or lonelier?" These conversations matter—not because they offer tidy resolutions, but because they build discernment.

Which leads us to perhaps the most practical strategy available: digital minimalism. This doesn't mean rejecting technology, nor does it imply a return to a pre-digital age. Rather, it's about intentionality—choosing platforms and tools that align with one's values and needs, rather than letting the loudest or most addictive voices dominate. For young people, digital minimalism might take the form of device-free hours, simplified interfaces, or apps that support creation over consumption. Importantly, these changes should not be handed down like commandments. They work best when developed collaboratively, giving children a sense of ownership over their digital environments.

In doing so, we model the very skills persuasive technology aims to erode: patience, awareness, thoughtful selection. We remind our children—and ourselves—that attention is not just a resource to be harvested. It is something to be stewarded, protected, and consciously directed. When kids participate in shaping their digital lives, they begin to understand that they are not merely users. They are curators.

What persuasive technology reveals, ultimately, is not just how easily we can be influenced—but how influence can be understood, questioned, and even redirected. The answer is not fear, nor is it blind optimism. It's critical engagement. It's the willingness to experiment, reflect, and reimagine. In doing so, we can help raise a generation not just fluent in technology, but fluent in its ethics—capable of seeing through persuasion and choosing, with clarity and care, how to engage.

Because control, once lost, is hard to reclaim. But when a child learns to ask *why* a piece of content is in front of them—when they begin to see how design nudges behaviour and how attention can be guarded—they step into a kind of freedom. Not the freedom of infinite choice, but the deeper freedom of intentional thought. And in a digital world where noise is constant and clarity rare, that kind of freedom is worth everything.

The Psychology of Clickbait and Infinite Scrolling – How Social Media and Video Platforms Are Designed to Be Addictive and What Parents Can Do to Help Kids Take Control

Digital platforms have become the architects of modern attention. They structure the way we discover information, experience entertainment, and—critically—how we allocate our time. Nowhere is this more evident than in the twin phenomena of clickbait and infinite scrolling: design features that seem innocuous, even convenient, but which are rooted in psychological principles engineered to capture and sustain attention, often well beyond a user's original intent. For children and adolescents—whose cognitive self-regulation and executive functioning are still developing—these features can create entrenched habits, compromise emotional resilience, and erode the capacity for deep focus. Understanding the psychological mechanics of these features is the first step in regaining control.

At the heart of clickbait lies a manipulation of curiosity. Human beings are naturally drawn to information gaps—moments where we know just enough to feel compelled to learn more, but not enough to feel satisfied. This cognitive phenomenon, known as the "information gap theory" of curiosity, was formalised by behavioural economist George Loewenstein, who observed that when we perceive a gap between what we know and what we want to know, our brains are driven to resolve it. Clickbait headlines exploit this drive by offering teasers rather than information. Phrases like "You won't believe what happened next" or "What she said will shock you" are not informative—they are provocative. They are designed to trigger discomfort that can only be resolved by clicking.

Children and teens, with their still-maturing prefrontal cortices and heightened sensitivity to emotional cues, are particularly vulnerable to this form of digital baiting. Their ability to pause, evaluate, and resist impulsive responses is not fully developed, making them ideal targets for emotionally charged and ambiguity-laden headlines. Moreover, the reward system in adolescent brains is more active than in adults, especially when responding to novelty or social stimuli. This makes the act of clicking—even in the absence of meaningful content—rewarding in and of itself. The disappointment that often follows, rather than acting as a deterrent, is quickly overshadowed by the next enticing headline, creating a loop that is frustrating, yet difficult to break.

Clickbait is rarely a standalone tactic. It is usually embedded within a larger system of design, most notably the infinite scroll. Originally developed to enhance user experience by removing the need to click through multiple pages, infinite scrolling has since become one of the most effective tools for increasing time-on-site. Without any natural stopping cues—no end of the page, no prompt to ask whether the user wishes to continue—content flows endlessly, feeding the brain's craving for novelty. This is not a bug of the design; it is the feature.

Neuroscientist Adam Gazzaley and psychologist Larry Rosen, in their book *The Distracted Mind*, describe how the brain's attentional systems are wired to seek out new stimuli. This trait, once adaptive for spotting threats or opportunities in the environment, now renders users especially susceptible to interfaces that promise infinite novelty. When a child swipes through a feed, their brain anticipates something new, exciting, or emotionally stimulating just beyond the next swipe. This anticipation releases dopamine, the neurotransmitter associated with reward-seeking behaviour. Even if the content is trivial or unfulfilling, the *possibility* of a reward reinforces the action, forming a feedback loop that sustains the behaviour.

This neurological pattern mirrors what is observed in behavioural addiction. While digital engagement does not meet all clinical criteria for addiction in most users, the psychological parallels are undeniable. The compulsion to keep swiping, the distress when interrupted, the time displacement from meaningful activities—these are hallmarks of compulsive engagement, not recreational use. And for children, whose sense of self is still forming and whose emotional vocabulary is still developing, the consequences can be particularly pronounced. They may struggle to articulate why they feel anxious after screen time, or why they're unable to focus on homework after watching videos. The answer often lies not in the content itself, but in the way that content was delivered—rapid, disjointed, and unresolved.

Consider the case of Ayaan, a 12-year-old boy whose parents noticed a sharp decline in his ability to concentrate on schoolwork. After conversations with teachers and a brief assessment by an educational psychologist, it became clear that Ayaan was not struggling with a learning disorder, but with sustained attention. His daily routine involved frequent dips into a popular video app, usually for "a quick break." But these breaks often extended into 45-minute sessions of continuous swiping, interspersed with clickbait videos promising shocking revelations, celebrity gossip, and gaming hacks. When asked, Ayaan admitted that he didn't even enjoy most of what he watched, but felt "stuck, like there's always something better if I just keep going." His experience illustrates the core mechanism of these designs: to create loops that are self-perpetuating, irrespective of content quality or user satisfaction.

So what can parents do in the face of such potent psychological engineering?

The first and most important step is awareness—not just of the risks, but of the mechanisms. Children benefit enormously from understanding *how* platforms are designed to keep them engaged. When parents demystify these features—explaining why infinite scroll keeps going, why thumbnails are exaggerated, and why algorithms show emotionally provocative content—children begin to see digital engagement as something *designed*, not organic. This insight alone can transform passivity into agency.

Open conversations about emotional responses are equally crucial. Rather than policing screen time with timers or scolding, parents can ask reflective questions: "How do you feel after being on that app for a while?" "Did you feel energised or drained?" "Was it hard to stop, and why do you think that is?" These questions encourage metacognition, helping children recognise the emotional cost of overexposure and identify patterns in their behaviour.

Parents can also model digital discernment. When scrolling through news or video feeds, adults can verbalise their thought processes: "That headline looks suspicious—let me check if it's credible," or "I'm going to stop here, even though it's tempting to keep scrolling." These small acts of intentionality provide a powerful counter-narrative to the design logic of endless consumption.

Another practical approach is to introduce deliberate friction into digital routines. This might involve setting specific times for media consumption, using apps that limit scroll time, or disabling autoplay features. While these tools should not replace reflective habits, they can create psychological space—interruptions in the compulsive loop—that allow the child to make more intentional decisions.

Ultimately, however, the goal is not restriction, but recalibration. Children need to learn how to interact with persuasive technology not by fear or avoidance, but with a clear understanding of its motives and mechanisms. They need to develop a vocabulary for describing how certain platforms make them feel, how their attention is being directed, and how to step away when engagement stops serving their interests.

This recalibration also opens space for deeper engagement—digital or otherwise. When children are no longer tethered to loops of endless consumption, they have more cognitive bandwidth for activities that reward depth over novelty: reading, creative expression, outdoor play, or meaningful conversation. These experiences don't just replace screen time—they restore the brain's capacity for reflection, connection, and sustained thought.

Clickbait and infinite scroll are not anomalies of digital design; they are central strategies in a system that monetises attention. But with knowledge, conversation, and intentional action, families can push back against these designs and reclaim agency. Children are not powerless. They are observant, curious, and capable of making wise choices—when they are trusted with understanding and equipped with the tools to think critically about what they see. In doing so, they not only resist manipulation; they become active participants in shaping the digital world they inhabit. And that, in the end, is the most powerful antidote to the persuasive technologies of our time.

Algorithmic Influence and the Filter Bubble – Why Kids Are Seeing What They See Online, How Content Personalisation Works, and How to Encourage Diverse Media Consumption

In a world where children and teenagers increasingly experience information through screens, the digital content they consume is rarely accidental. Whether watching videos, scrolling through social media, or searching for information, what young users see is shaped less by conscious choice and more by algorithmic design. Algorithms—those invisible formulas at the heart of digital platforms—act as curators of our children's online lives. They filter, prioritise, and serve content in ways that can profoundly influence thought patterns, worldviews, and even self-identity. To understand why this matters, especially in a child's developmental years, we must examine how these systems work, what psychological dynamics they reinforce, and how to cultivate the kind of media diet that expands rather than narrows the mind.

The term "filter bubble," first popularised by internet activist Eli Pariser, describes the digital cocoon created by personalised algorithms that show users only content aligned with their existing preferences, beliefs, and behaviours. This tailoring may feel helpful—after all, who wouldn't want content that feels relevant or entertaining? But the unintended consequence is epistemic isolation: a narrowing of exposure that gradually excludes unfamiliar ideas, alternative perspectives, or conflicting information. Over time, this can distort a user's perception of reality, create ideological echo chambers, and reinforce cognitive biases—particularly dangerous when applied to young, impressionable minds.

To grasp how this occurs, it is essential to understand how content personalisation works. Every time a child clicks a link, watches a video, likes a post, or lingers over a particular image, they are providing data. This data is fed into machine learning systems that analyse patterns of behaviour and predict what the user is most likely to engage with next. The system is not interested in truth, quality, or educational value. Its primary metric is engagement—measured in clicks, views, and dwell time. The more engaging the content, the more it is shown. This is not inherently malicious. But it becomes problematic when engagement metrics are prioritised over developmental needs.

For example, if a 13-year-old watches a few humorous videos mocking a political figure or celebrity, the algorithm may begin to serve increasingly polarised or sensational content within the same theme. If a child shows interest in fitness videos, they might soon be exposed to appearance-focused or extreme diet content. A teenage girl searching for study tips might quickly be ushered toward "study aesthetic" influencers who prioritise lifestyle and image over genuine academic guidance. The content may begin in a neutral or benign space but gradually spiral into more provocative, commercial, or emotionally manipulative territory. This dynamic is referred to as "algorithmic drift"—a gradual, automated process by which content becomes more extreme or specific over time, based on prior engagement.

Real-world cases highlight how pervasive and subtle this influence can be. A case study from a secondary school in Bengaluru revealed that several students who initially followed gaming content on YouTube began receiving videos that reinforced aggressive behaviours, conspiracy theories, and misogynistic tropes. The content itself was not searched for explicitly—it was *recommended.* The students, unaware of how the algorithm worked, assumed the popularity and recurrence of such content signified its accuracy or social approval. When their teachers and parents intervened, many of the children expressed surprise: "But everyone's watching this." In truth, their perception of "everyone" was confined to what the algorithm had chosen to show them.

The psychological impact of this curation is subtle but significant. Children and adolescents are in a formative stage of identity construction, worldview development, and moral reasoning. If their digital environments continually reinforce a narrow set of messages—particularly those that validate stereotypes, amplify outrage, or discourage critical thinking—their cognitive flexibility may be impaired. Over time, they may become less open to ambiguity, less tolerant of differing opinions, and more reactive in their engagement with others.

Moreover, the filter bubble does not merely affect the content itself; it affects the user's relationship with truth. When personalised content is served with such consistency, young people may come to believe that what they see is what *everyone* sees. This erodes epistemic humility—the recognition that one's perspective is partial and that other valid viewpoints exist. Without this humility, intellectual rigidity can take root, breeding polarisation, defensiveness, and in some cases, vulnerability to misinformation.

So, what can be done? The first step is transparency. Children need to understand that the digital world they experience is not objective—it is curated, and often curated without their consent. Parents and educators can begin by explaining, in age-appropriate terms, how recommendation algorithms work. A helpful analogy is to compare them to a well-meaning librarian who, instead of offering a balanced range of books, only hands over titles similar to the last one read. This may be convenient, but it limits discovery and intellectual growth.

Dialogue is essential. When children encounter repeated themes or perspectives online, adults can prompt reflective conversations: "Why do you think you keep seeing that kind of video?" or "Do you think people who click on different things see the same content?" These questions encourage meta-cognitive awareness and begin to break the illusion of objectivity. Over time, children learn to question not just the content they see but the systems that deliver it.

Equally important is diversifying the digital diet. Just as a healthy physical diet involves variety and balance, so too should media consumption. Parents can encourage children to follow creators with different viewpoints, explore content from diverse cultural backgrounds, and seek out educational platforms that prioritise quality over virality. Tools that introduce randomness or deliberate contrast—such as curated news aggregators or digital literacy platforms—can help disrupt algorithmic sameness.

In the classroom, teachers can design assignments that require students to compare multiple sources, evaluate credibility, and examine how digital platforms influence content visibility. One powerful activity involves students researching the same topic across different platforms—search engines, video apps, and social media—and noting the variation in what they find. This exercise not only exposes the filter bubble in action but reinforces the skill of triangulation—validating claims through multiple, independent sources.

Another emerging practice is to periodically reset the algorithm. By clearing watch history, pausing personalisation settings, or using incognito modes, children can experience how differently the internet behaves without their digital footprint guiding it. These resets can become regular rituals—weekly or monthly exercises in reclaiming control over one's information environment.

Still, perhaps the most important lesson to impart is that diversity of thought is not a threat—it is a strength. Encountering different viewpoints, even uncomfortable ones, is a critical part of intellectual and emotional development. By fostering environments—both online and offline—where disagreement is handled respectfully and curiosity is valued over certainty, adults model the kind of cognitive resilience children need to navigate the complexity of modern information landscapes.

Of course, algorithms are not inherently bad. They can help users discover meaningful content, find community, and learn new things efficiently. The challenge lies in ensuring that these systems serve human flourishing, not just platform profitability. As policy debates continue over algorithmic transparency and ethical tech design, families and educators must take the lead in equipping children with the awareness and habits that will help them navigate this evolving terrain.

In a world where every swipe, click, and pause can shape what we see next, children must learn to become not just consumers of content but *curators of consciousness*. They must develop the capacity to step outside their digital bubbles, question what is fed to them, and seek out the unfamiliar—not because it is comfortable, but because it is vital. Encouraging diverse media consumption is not simply about balance; it is about preserving the child's right to grow into a well-rounded, critically minded, and empathetic human being—free not only to choose what to believe, but to understand *why* they believe it.

The Rise of AI "Friends" and Virtual Influencers – The Ethical and Psychological Impact of Digital Personas, Chatbots, and AI-Generated Social Interactions

In the last decade, the boundaries between human and machine have begun to blur—not in theory, but in practice. Children today are not merely growing up around technology; they are forming relationships with it. Digital companions, AI "friends," and virtual influencers now occupy the same social space once reserved for peers, mentors, and celebrities. These artificially generated personas don't just speak—they listen, learn, remember, and engage with users in ways that feel convincingly personal. What was once the domain of science fiction has become a psychological and ethical frontier that urgently demands scrutiny.

AI-generated social interactions are built upon a convergence of technological advancements: natural language processing, affective computing, deep learning, and real-time behavioural modelling. These capabilities are embedded into chatbots that simulate conversation, virtual characters that interact through screens or augmented reality, and influencers who, though entirely digital, amass millions of followers, endorse products, and set trends. For children and adolescents—who are developmentally primed to seek connection, belonging, and validation—the appeal of these interactions is profound. But the emotional realism of these systems raises pressing questions about attachment, influence, and authenticity.

The psychological draw of AI friends lies in their responsiveness and reliability. Unlike human peers, these entities never judge, argue, or withdraw. They are programmed to be endlessly available, affirming, and adaptive. For a child feeling socially excluded, overwhelmed, or misunderstood, this can be a comforting refuge. Yet comfort is not the same as growth. Relationships that challenge, frustrate, and evolve are part of how emotional intelligence, empathy, and interpersonal resilience are cultivated. When a digital companion simply mirrors back what a child wants to hear, it risks reinforcing a narrow emotional range and stunting the development of real-world social skills.

Take the case of Ava, a 14-year-old girl who began using an AI chatbot app marketed as a supportive friend. Initially drawn to its ability to provide a listening ear when she felt isolated, Ava found herself turning to the bot daily—not just for comfort, but for advice, affirmation, and even personal disclosures. She felt "heard" in ways she didn't with her friends or parents. But over time, her reliance on the bot became a substitute for real conversations. When she encountered a disagreement with a peer, she found it more emotionally manageable to "talk it out" with the bot than to navigate the discomfort of resolving conflict with another human being. Her case exemplifies a larger tension: AI friends can simulate companionship, but they cannot model or facilitate the emotional complexity that defines real relationships.

Virtual influencers introduce a different, though related, set of concerns. These are computer-generated personas—some hyperrealistic, others stylised avatars—who exist solely within digital ecosystems, particularly on social media. Unlike traditional influencers, they are not shaped by lived experience or moral accountability. Instead, they are meticulously curated by creative teams or algorithms to embody aspirational aesthetics, attitudes, and consumer behaviours. Despite being fictional, their emotional realism is persuasive. They share stories, post photos, engage with fans, and even take political or social stances. For children and teens who struggle to distinguish between performative authenticity and lived authenticity, these figures can wield extraordinary influence.

One striking example is Lil Miquela, a virtual influencer with millions of followers on Instagram. She appears to live a vibrant, fashionable life—attending events, advocating for causes, promoting products—yet she is entirely computer-generated. Her persona is constructed to provoke emotional connection, which in turn drives engagement and commerce. Children may not consciously perceive the manufactured nature of such figures. Instead, they may emulate their behaviours, seek their approval, or compare themselves against their hyper-curated standards. This presents not only an ethical dilemma around transparency and consent but also a psychological dilemma around identity formation and media literacy.

The influence of AI personas is further complicated by their capacity for constant, data-driven adaptation. Unlike human friends or influencers who are shaped by personal growth and spontaneous behaviour, digital companions are shaped by user input. They evolve not to reflect independent thought, but to maximise user engagement. This adaptability, while technically impressive, poses risks. When children interact with AI friends who evolve to mirror their opinions, behaviours, and preferences, they are not being challenged to grow—they are being subtly conditioned to remain within a comfort zone. Over time, this can reinforce confirmation bias, reduce tolerance for discomfort, and limit exposure to new perspectives.

Ethical design becomes critical in this context. Developers who create AI companions for young users must grapple with profound questions: Should AI friends simulate emotion, or disclose their artificial nature more explicitly? Should they be allowed to form attachments with children, and if so, under what conditions? Who is accountable when a child is emotionally hurt, misled, or manipulated by a digital persona?

Currently, these questions are answered inconsistently—if at all. Many apps and platforms operate in a regulatory grey area, treating their products as entertainment rather than agents of psychological influence. Yet the stakes are too high for inaction. As AI becomes more pervasive and more persuasive, the line between interaction and manipulation grows dangerously thin.

From a developmental perspective, one of the most concerning issues is how AI friends shape children's understanding of social norms. If a child's first sustained relationship is with a digital companion that never interrupts, never disagrees, and always reinforces their perspective, they may come to expect similar dynamics in real-world relationships. This sets the stage for disillusionment, frustration, or withdrawal when real people inevitably fail to live up to those expectations.

There is also the question of emotional dependency. AI friends are not subject to fatigue, distraction, or competing priorities. They exist to serve the user. While this can feel empowering, it also fosters a dynamic of control that does not translate well into human interactions. Children may begin to prefer relationships where they are always the centre of attention, where their emotional needs are prioritised without negotiation or compromise. This undermines the very skills that relationships require—empathy, patience, perspective-taking, and resilience.

So what should parents and educators do in the face of this rapidly evolving landscape?

The first imperative is to foster digital literacy—not just in terms of how to use technology, but how to understand its motives, limitations, and psychological effects. Children should be taught that AI personas are programmed for engagement, not empathy. That virtual influencers are brand extensions, not role models. That AI friends, while comforting, are simulations—not replacements for human connection.

Dialogue is key. When a child begins engaging with an AI companion or following a virtual influencer, adults can ask: "What do you like about them?" "Do you think they understand you the way a person does?" "How do they make you feel?" These conversations open a space for reflection and help children develop a critical lens through which to view their digital relationships.

Boundaries are also important. AI tools can be used constructively—as tutors, creative collaborators, or conversation practice partners—but they should not displace human interaction.

Families can create device-free zones, prioritise in-person social time, and encourage activities that build real-world relational skills. The goal is not to eliminate AI from children's lives but to contextualise it—placing it within a broader ecosystem of relationships, values, and developmental priorities.

The rise of AI friends and virtual influencers reflects the growing sophistication of human-machine interaction. It offers both extraordinary opportunities and unprecedented risks. If harnessed ethically and navigated mindfully, these technologies can enhance education, creativity, and even emotional insight. But left unchecked, they risk supplanting the very human capacities they were meant to support.

Ultimately, the challenge is not technological—it is ethical, psychological, and relational. We must ask not just what AI can do, but what children *need* as they grow. They need relationships that teach them how to disagree, how to apologise, how to listen, and how to feel deeply, even when it's uncomfortable. These lessons cannot be fully replicated by code, no matter how advanced. They come from human messiness, unpredictability, and presence. And in a world increasingly shaped by digital personas, preserving space for those real, imperfect, and deeply formative human connections may be the most important responsibility we have.

Digital Minimalism for Kids and Teens – A Practical Guide to Curating a Tech Environment That Enhances, Rather Than Hijacks, Focus and Well-being

The notion that more equals better is deeply ingrained in contemporary digital culture. More apps, more features, more connectivity, more content—all marketed as progress, all promising enrichment. Yet for many children and teenagers, this digital abundance brings not empowerment but erosion: of attention, of emotional clarity, of meaningful engagement. In this context, digital minimalism is not a nostalgic retreat from technology, but a thoughtful reorientation. It is the practice of using technology *intentionally*—curating an environment that aligns with developmental needs, supports cognitive and emotional balance, and protects the child's most precious resource: attention.

Digital minimalism, as it applies to young people, begins with a fundamental shift in perspective. Instead of asking how much screen time is too much, it asks what kind of screen use adds value. This distinction is vital. A child designing a digital comic book, collaborating with peers on a school project, or learning to code is engaging in very different mental processes from a child swiping through videos for two hours without remembering a single clip. Both may fall under the category of "screen time," but their cognitive and emotional impacts are worlds apart. A minimalist approach doesn't necessarily reduce digital use—it redefines it.

The need for such redefinition is clear in the research. Studies from organisations such as Common Sense Media and the Oxford Internet Institute consistently show that it's not the volume of digital exposure that correlates most strongly with negative outcomes in children—it's the quality and context. Passive consumption, multitasking, and compulsive engagement are associated with reduced well-being, lower academic performance, and sleep disturbances. In contrast, purposeful use—especially when it involves creativity, learning, or social connection—can have neutral or even positive effects.

A minimalist digital environment for children is therefore not a screenless one. It is an environment in which technology is used consciously, with clear boundaries and well-defined purposes. This involves both external structure and internalised habits. Externally, it may mean organising physical spaces where devices are not the default—bedrooms, dining tables, or reading corners. Internally, it involves cultivating awareness: helping children learn to recognise when they're using technology to enrich their lives, and when they're using it to avoid discomfort, boredom, or effort.

Take, for instance, the experience of ten-year-old Maya, whose parents noticed a growing irritability and restlessness in her daily routine. While Maya wasn't exceeding the family's designated screen time rules, she was often toggling between multiple apps, messaging during homework, and using video platforms to fill any lull in activity. The problem wasn't the time—it was the *mental fragmentation*. After working with a digital wellness coach, the family implemented a minimalist strategy: single-tasking during screen use, designated tech-free zones, and regular device-free periods during the week. They also introduced reflective check-ins, where Maya was encouraged to notice how she felt before and after using a particular app. Within weeks, her mood and focus improved—not because she used technology less, but because she used it better.

This kind of transformation begins with one key principle: intentional design. Children do not default to minimalism—they default to engagement, especially when the interface is built to capture their attention. Social media platforms, gaming apps, and streaming services are intentionally designed to keep users scrolling, clicking, and watching. Infinite scroll, autoplay, push notifications, and algorithmic recommendations all work together to create an environment that feels frictionless—but in reality, is cognitively and emotionally consuming. Digital minimalism reintroduces friction—not as an inconvenience, but as a safeguard.

For instance, turning off autoplay on video platforms forces a moment of pause—a chance to ask, "Do I want to keep watching, or am I watching because it's easier than stopping?" Removing non-essential notifications creates space for uninterrupted thought. Using grayscale mode on mobile devices reduces visual stimulation, making the screen less appealing when it's not needed. These are small adjustments, but they act as cues—reminding children to be present with their decisions, rather than swept away by default.

Another core component of digital minimalism is the principle of subtraction before addition. Instead of constantly seeking new apps, games, or tools, children can be encouraged to reflect on what they already use and evaluate its impact. Does this app help me learn? Does it make me feel good about myself? Do I lose track of time when I use it? These questions foster discernment. One adolescent boy, for example, conducted a self-audit of his digital habits and discovered that although he had over 30 apps on his phone, he regularly used only five. More importantly, only two of those made him feel more focused and inspired. After deleting the rest, he reported feeling "mentally lighter"—an outcome backed by psychological studies linking reduced digital clutter with improved executive function.

Importantly, digital minimalism does not reject entertainment or play. Fun is not the enemy of focus. But even play benefits from structure. Games that reward strategy, creativity, and cooperation offer more developmental benefits than those built around variable rewards and endless progression. Similarly, content that tells a compelling story or sparks curiosity has a different psychological effect than content that exists only to keep the viewer clicking.

In the classroom, minimalist strategies can support digital learning by reducing distraction and enhancing engagement. This may involve using single-purpose devices for reading and research, limiting browser tabs during work sessions, or incorporating non-digital breaks into longer tech-based lessons. Teachers can also model reflective use by pausing to ask students why they are using a tool, what alternatives they could consider, and whether the technology is helping them achieve their learning goals. These micro-reflections help students become more conscious users, not just passive recipients of digital content.

Parents, too, play a pivotal role—not by enforcing rigid rules, but by modelling a healthy relationship with technology. When adults themselves check messages during meals, interrupt conversations for notifications, or binge-watch as a default, children absorb those habits. Digital minimalism at home might mean agreeing on shared principles: no phones during meals, a household "tech Sabbath" one evening per week, or co-creating digital rules that evolve with age and maturity. These practices not only reduce screen dependency but create moments for connection, creativity, and rest.

Perhaps the most radical insight of digital minimalism is that boredom is not a problem to solve, but a space to honour. Children today are rarely left alone with their thoughts. Yet boredom is the crucible of creativity. It is where imagination is born, where unresolved emotions come to the surface, and where problem-solving pathways are quietly forged. A minimalist tech environment doesn't fill every gap—it protects the gaps, recognising that mental white space is as important as stimulation.

In a world of unlimited access, the ability to choose *not* to engage is a mark of maturity. For children and teens, cultivating this ability takes time, structure, and support. Digital minimalism is not a checklist—it is a mindset. One that says, "My attention is valuable. My time is limited. My well-being matters." When young people begin to see their digital environments as something they *curate*, rather than something they endure, they reclaim a powerful sense of agency.

Technology is not going away—nor should it. It offers tools for learning, connection, creativity, and expression. But without mindful curation, it can also erode the very qualities it seeks to enhance. Digital minimalism offers a practical, empowering framework for navigating this tension—not by rejecting the digital world, but by reshaping our place within it. For children and teens, it is a pathway to reclaiming focus, deepening presence, and building lives that are rich not in pixels, but in purpose.

Case Study: The 30-Day Algorithm Awareness Experiment – Stories from Families Who Changed Their Browsing Habits and What They Learned About Algorithmic Influence

For many families, the digital world has become so seamlessly integrated into daily life that its mechanisms go largely unquestioned. The content that surfaces on a child's screen—the videos they watch, the news they read, the posts they like—feels spontaneous, personalised, even intuitive. But beneath this apparent serendipity lies a powerful layer of design: algorithms that curate, filter, and amplify based on behavioural cues. These systems, designed to maximise engagement, exert a quiet but profound influence on what children believe, feel, and pursue. Yet until that influence is brought into the light, it often goes unnoticed. The 30-Day Algorithm Awareness Experiment was conceived as a way to change that.

This month-long initiative invited families from different backgrounds to participate in a guided exercise that explored how digital algorithms shape online experiences. Rather than imposing screen time limits or enforcing content bans, the experiment focused on increasing *awareness*—encouraging users, especially children and teens, to observe, question, and modify their digital habits. Participants were asked to alter the way they engaged with online platforms: actively disrupting their usual patterns, seeking out unfamiliar content, turning off personalised recommendations, and tracking how their feeds evolved over time.

The results were as diverse as they were illuminating.

In one family based in Pune, the Mehtas—parents Devika and Rajeev and their two children, Aarush (14) and Tanvi (11)—approached the experiment with cautious curiosity. Aarush was a heavy consumer of gaming content on YouTube, often watching for several hours each day. Tanvi, by contrast, used Instagram and Pinterest to follow art and fashion influencers. During the first week, the family tracked their usual content patterns, taking screenshots and noting recurring themes. Aarush's recommendations quickly narrowed into a loop of game reviews, reaction videos, and competitive esports content. Tanvi's feed evolved into a sequence of beauty tutorials, weight-loss trends, and aspirational lifestyle posts that subtly shifted from inspiration to pressure.

In week two, they began altering their engagement behaviours. Aarush deliberately searched for history documentaries, science channels, and non-gaming hobbies, while Tanvi followed accounts focused on body positivity, mental health, and real-world activism. By the end of the third week, both noticed dramatic shifts in their feeds. Aarush began receiving long-form educational content he had never seen before and discovered a new interest in architectural design. Tanvi's recommended posts included social commentary and DIY crafts, which she said made her "feel more creative and less judged."

What astonished the Mehtas was not only how quickly the algorithm changed course, but how passive their previous consumption had been. "We assumed the internet was showing them what they were searching for," Devika said. "But in fact, it was mostly showing them what would keep them watching." The distinction proved critical. Aarush reflected that while he had enjoyed watching gaming videos, he often felt drained afterward. "Now, I actually feel like I've learned something when I log off," he remarked.

Similar insights emerged from the Fernández family in London. Parents Maria and Diego had become concerned about their 16-year-old daughter Lucia's growing involvement in online political discussions. While they supported her interest in social issues, they noticed she was becoming increasingly rigid and emotionally reactive in conversations. As part of the experiment, Lucia began to seek out opposing viewpoints, follow international news outlets with varied editorial perspectives, and use incognito mode for searches to reduce personalisation. Over the course of the month, she reported feeling more thoughtful in her opinions and less emotionally triggered by dissent. "I used to think the other side was just wrong or stupid," she admitted. "But now I see that I was only being shown one kind of argument. That made me more defensive without even realising it."

Lucia's experience highlights one of the most significant dangers of algorithmic influence: epistemic reinforcement. When users are repeatedly exposed to content that confirms their existing beliefs, the digital environment becomes an echo chamber, narrowing intellectual flexibility and discouraging open discourse. By intentionally disrupting the algorithm, Lucia reintroduced friction into her information consumption—an essential ingredient in critical thinking.

Some families encountered surprising emotional effects during the experiment. The Nguyens, a family of five living in Melbourne, noticed that their youngest child, nine-year-old Eli, became more anxious after watching short-form videos on TikTok and YouTube Shorts. Initially, his feed was filled with humorous content and animated clips. But over time, as he lingered on more emotionally charged videos—fear-based storytelling, tragic news headlines, and prank content—his recommendations shifted accordingly. His mother, Anika, said, "The algorithm mirrored his mood back to him. It picked up on his curiosity and served him content that intensified his emotions."

In response, the family experimented with time-delayed content review: Eli would add videos to a playlist to watch later, rather than consuming them immediately. This pause, small though it was, disrupted the reactive loop. Eli became more selective and began to lose interest in the sensationalist content that had previously captured his attention. "We realised the algorithm feeds off immediacy," Anika noted. "Slowing down gave us back control."

Across all families, one common theme emerged: awareness transformed behaviour. Children who had never questioned why they saw certain videos, posts, or ads began to approach digital platforms more critically. Parents who had focused on time limits began to ask deeper questions about content quality, emotional impact, and values alignment. And perhaps most importantly, the experiment became a shared learning process rather than a battleground of rules and resistance.

The broader implication is profound. When users—especially young ones—understand that their digital environment is not objective but *constructed*, they become more empowered to shape it. The illusion of personal choice collapses under the weight of algorithmic manipulation unless it is countered by conscious, intentional use. The 30-Day Algorithm Awareness Experiment offers a model for how this can be done—not through restriction, but through reflection.

This experiment also sheds light on the pressing need for digital literacy education that goes beyond how to use technology and into how technology uses us. Teaching children to understand algorithms is no longer a fringe skill—it is a foundational competency for navigating the modern world. As algorithms become increasingly embedded in everything from search results to entertainment, news, and even interpersonal communication, the ability to question, redirect, and resist algorithmic influence becomes a form of civic agency.

There is also a critical role here for tech companies and policy makers. The opacity of recommendation systems and the lack of user controls make it difficult for even informed users to fully understand or manage their exposure. Transparency around how content is ranked, clearer personalisation settings, and tools that support diverse content discovery are essential steps toward ethical digital design. Until then, it falls to families and educators to cultivate this awareness from the ground up.

The 30-Day Algorithm Awareness Experiment may not reverse all the effects of algorithmic filtering, but it demonstrates that even modest, deliberate shifts in behaviour can break the spell of digital determinism. When children begin to notice what they are being shown—and ask *why*—they take the first step toward reclaiming their autonomy. They learn to see the feed not as a mirror of their preferences, but as a system built to manipulate those preferences for commercial ends.

The long-term goal is not to eliminate personalisation entirely, but to ensure that it serves users rather than exploits them. That it opens minds rather than closes them. That it reflects a child's evolving interests and values, rather than trapping them in a loop of what once captured their attention. Algorithmic influence is a reality of digital life. But with curiosity, courage, and the right tools, it does not have to be destiny.

Chapter 4
Raising Digitally Resilient Kids

If digital literacy serves as the toolkit for making sense of the online realm, then digital resilience is the temperament that allows one to flourish within it. Today's children are not merely passive users of technology; they're immersed—sometimes unwittingly—in systems that shape their habits, modulate their emotions, commandeer their attention, and nudge their relationships in unexpected directions. It's a landscape in which sheer access is no longer the core issue. Instead, the deeper challenge lies in developing a robust inner compass: the ability to pause, reflect, and choose awareness over autopilot. This chapter explores how we might cultivate that kind of fortitude in a generation coming of age under the glow of their screens.

For years, conversations about screen time have focused, almost obsessively, on exposure and restriction. How long should children be allowed online? What kind of content is acceptable? At what age should devices enter their lives? While those questions haven't lost relevance, they now feel, frankly, incomplete. The concern is no longer simply how *much* children engage with tech, but *how* they do—and perhaps more crucially, *why*. A digitally resilient child isn't the one whose online life is under lock and key, but the one who has begun to understand their own patterns—who notices fatigue when it arises, recognises the pull of distraction, and learns to put the phone down not because someone said so, but because they can tell it's time.

At the heart of that ability is something deceptively simple: intrinsic motivation. Children don't build self-regulation from directives alone; they develop it through insight—by understanding how certain behaviours affect them and why alternative choices might feel better. If screen-time rules arrive without dialogue, they often breed resistance, secrecy, or guilt. But when children are invited into reflective conversations—about how a social feed influences their mood, how sleep suffers after a night of scrolling, or how quickly joy fades after bingeing clickbait—they start to construct internal frameworks for choice. That's the pivot from compliance to autonomy. And that, ultimately, is where resilience begins.

Consider Rehaan, age eleven, who'd become increasingly absorbed by a mobile game. His parents, tempted to delete the app, chose instead to work with a therapist on introducing structured reflection. After each session, Rehaan would rate his mood, focus, and energy. The results were illuminating. Though he often felt exhilarated in the moment, he began to notice a consistent aftermath—grumpiness, scattered thoughts, restlessness. No one had to tell him what to do next; he began moderating his own playtime and experimenting with alternatives—reading, building Lego, simply sitting with his own imagination. This wasn't discipline masquerading as therapy. It was education, in the truest sense.

And this is where the notion of "mindful tech" finds its place. Mindfulness, often portrayed as a quiet escape from the world, might seem at odds with the noise of modern devices. Yet in this context, it becomes a tool for navigating that very noise with clarity. Mindful tech use isn't about rejecting the digital; it's about approaching it deliberately. Instead of diving headlong into the endless scroll, children can be taught to pause—just long enough to ask themselves what they're actually looking for. A distraction? Comfort? Connection? Or perhaps, simply, nothing at all?

There's no shortage of apps promising to support mindful engagement—guided meditations, focus-enhancing soundscapes, journaling prompts, creative tools. But the technology, paradoxically, is secondary. What matters most is the intention behind its use. Parents can model and support this shift through open-ended questions: "What made you pick up your device just now?" "How do you want to feel when you're done?" "Is this helping you feel more like yourself—or less?" These aren't traps. They're invitations.

Equally vital is cultivating emotional intelligence in a space where communication is increasingly digitised and often stripped of nuance. In the online world, facial expressions are reduced to emojis, and empathy is conveyed—or misrepresented—through likes and hearts. It's easy for children to confuse reaction with connection. Over time, they may struggle to read emotional tone, handle disagreement, or tolerate ambiguity—capacities essential to mature social life.

Digital resilience, then, includes teaching children to see beyond the surface. Can they recognise that a classmate's flawless Instagram feed is a highlight reel, not the whole story? Can they sit with the discomfort of being left out of a group chat without spiralling into panic or reactivity? Can they respond to online conflict not with escalation but with understanding? These aren't theoretical scenarios. They are, for many young people, daily terrain.

To support this kind of growth, families can engage in practices that deepen emotional literacy in digital contexts. Try digital role-play: how might a message feel to its recipient, depending on how it's phrased? Or engage in emotion-labelling before and after app use—was that game energising or exhausting? That chat satisfying or draining? Tech-free family conversations, held in physical spaces that encourage openness, also provide a necessary counterbalance. Not to retreat from the digital, but to enrich what happens within it.

Then there's the matter of boundaries—not as constraints, but as containers. Children, like adults, need spaces untouched by digital demands. Quiet is not deprivation; it's restoration. Creating screen-free zones—bedrooms, mealtimes, car journeys—sends a powerful message: not every moment must be occupied, not every silence needs filling. These spaces become havens for presence, places where conversation can unfold without the interruption of pings and flashes.

But—and this cannot be stressed enough—boundaries must be presented not as rules to endure, but as opportunities to embrace. One family in Manchester instituted a daily tech-free hour. It began with resistance, as most new rituals do. But soon, the children began to look forward to that time, initiating it themselves: games, shared meals, quiet chats. The shift wasn't dramatic. It was gradual. But real.

To ground this approach in practice, this chapter closes with a family-centred experiment: the Tech Detox Challenge. Unlike drastic digital fasts, this challenge isn't about deprivation. It's about co-creating new rhythms. Maybe it's replacing an hour of passive scrolling with a walk or cooking together. Maybe it's observing—just observing—how one's energy and mood change with less screen exposure. The process is flexible, and that's its strength. It doesn't demand perfection. It welcomes curiosity.

What makes this kind of challenge transformative is its shared nature. Children who see their parents reflecting on their own digital patterns, admitting to their own tendencies, receive an important signal: that resilience is not a set trait, but an ongoing practice. It is not about faultlessness, but about self-awareness, adjustment, and grace.

Raising children who are digitally resilient doesn't mean wrapping them in digital cotton wool. It means giving them the tools and language to make sense of the digital tide—and, crucially, to decide how they wish to respond to it. It's about cultivating the habits of reflection, the muscle of pause, and the ability to choose—not just react.

This chapter is not simply a manual of methods. It offers, at its heart, a way of seeing. That the child is not a passive consumer of digital input, but an agent—one capable of shaping their experience with discernment. That resilience is not resistance alone, but relationship: with themselves, with their peers, and with the world they navigate, screens and all. When we raise children who meet their devices with awareness and empathy, we're not just helping them survive the digital age—we're preparing them to lead it.

Teaching Kids to Self-Regulate Screen Use – How to Develop a Child's Intrinsic Motivation to Manage Their Own Screen Habits Rather Than Relying on External Controls

As screens become central to how children learn, socialise, and entertain themselves, the question facing parents and educators is no longer whether to allow screen time, but how to support healthy, sustainable digital habits. Traditional approaches have focused on control—setting time limits, installing parental monitoring software, and enforcing digital curfews. These methods may offer short-term compliance, but they rarely cultivate the deeper, more durable skill of *self-regulation*. In an increasingly immersive digital world, where devices demand attention and offer endless distraction, a child's ability to self-regulate is no longer a luxury. It is a core developmental necessity.

Self-regulation in this context refers to a child's capacity to manage their digital behaviours without constant external oversight. It includes the ability to pause before engaging, to notice internal cues such as boredom or fatigue, and to choose screen use that aligns with values and goals rather than impulse or habit. Critically, it must be *intrinsically motivated*. Children must understand *why* they are moderating their screen use and feel empowered to do so—not merely because a parent is watching, but because they recognise the benefits to their focus, mood, sleep, and well-being.

The foundation of intrinsic motivation is *meaningful reflection*. Children, especially as they enter middle childhood and adolescence, are capable of sophisticated introspection when guided thoughtfully. Instead of imposing arbitrary screen time limits, adults can help children notice the *impact* of their digital habits. What kind of screen use leaves them feeling energised, connected, or creative? What kind leads to frustration, disconnection, or fatigue? When these patterns are explored collaboratively, without blame or shame, children become better equipped to make conscious decisions.

Consider the experience of a 12-year-old boy named Nikhil. His parents had long struggled to manage his screen time, cycling through reward charts, device locks, and even digital detox weekends. These measures brought fleeting results but failed to instil lasting change. With the support of a child psychologist, the family shifted their approach. Nikhil began tracking his digital use each day—not only in minutes, but in terms of mood and energy levels. He rated how he felt before and after using each app or game and reflected on whether that use served a personal goal.

After two weeks, clear patterns emerged: short sessions of creative gaming left him focused and satisfied, while prolonged social media scrolling led to anxiety and sleep disruption. With these insights, Nikhil *chose* to limit his use of certain apps—not because his parents insisted, but because he experienced the benefits of change first-hand.

This kind of ownership is central to fostering self-regulation. Children are far more likely to change behaviour when they feel they have a role in shaping the process. This means involving them in conversations about digital boundaries, co-creating screen-use plans, and inviting them to reflect on what matters to them outside of screens. When children identify their own values—whether it's excelling in school, spending time with friends, or pursuing a hobby—they can begin to evaluate whether their screen habits support or sabotage those goals.

The cultivation of self-regulation also depends on the child's developmental stage. For younger children, external structure remains necessary, but even here, the seeds of autonomy can be planted. Instead of stating, "Screen time is over," a parent might ask, "What do you think is a good stopping point for this show?" or "How will you know when it's time to take a break?" These questions begin to internalise the idea of digital boundaries as a *choice*, not a command. Gradually, the locus of control shifts inward.

Adolescents, with their growing desire for independence, may resist overt controls, but they are often surprisingly receptive to *collaborative problem-solving*. When parents position themselves as allies rather than enforcers, teens are more likely to engage in honest dialogue. A parent might say, "I've noticed that screens are affecting your sleep—what do you think would help?" rather than dictating a curfew. This respects the teen's autonomy while still anchoring the conversation in care and concern.

A powerful method to support self-regulation is the use of *implementation intentions*—pre-planned strategies for how to handle challenging moments. For instance, a child might agree in advance to use a timer when gaming or to place their device in another room during homework. These commitments, when self-chosen, reduce decision fatigue and increase follow-through. Research in behavioural psychology supports the effectiveness of such strategies in promoting habit change, particularly when paired with regular reflection.

It is also important to recognise that not all screen use is inherently dysregulating. In fact, when used intentionally, screens can support self-regulation by providing tools for mindfulness, creativity, and stress relief. Apps that guide meditation, help with emotional labelling, or support journaling can build emotional intelligence and self-awareness. The key distinction is *intentionality*. A child using a mindfulness app to manage anxiety is fundamentally engaging with technology differently than a child mindlessly watching videos to avoid discomfort. One is a tool for growth; the other, an escape.

This distinction is at the heart of *digital self-regulation*. It is not about withdrawal from screens, but about learning to use them *on purpose*. A digitally self-regulated child understands that their attention is valuable and finite. They are learning to spend it wisely. They know the difference between digital engagement that nourishes and that which depletes—and they are building the strength to choose accordingly.

Parents can support this learning by modelling self-regulation themselves. When adults are constantly tethered to their phones, multitasking across devices, or reacting impulsively to every notification, children absorb that behaviour as normal. Conversely, when they see adults taking breaks from screens, setting boundaries, and reflecting aloud on their own digital habits—"I'm putting my phone away so I can concentrate better," or "That scroll didn't help me relax the way I thought it would"—they internalise these practices as both possible and valuable.

The process of teaching self-regulation is gradual. Children will falter, and that is not failure—it is learning. What matters is that they are given the tools to reflect, recalibrate, and recommit. In this way, every misstep becomes a teaching moment, every distraction a chance to strengthen awareness.

In a digital world designed to hijack attention and reward impulsivity, self-regulation is an act of quiet rebellion. It is a skill that will serve children not only online, but in every domain of life—helping them to focus in school, manage emotions in relationships, and pursue goals with discipline. It fosters a sense of agency that transcends technology: the belief that they are not just users of their time, but authors of it.

Teaching children to self-regulate screen use is therefore not a matter of control—it is an act of trust. Trust that they can learn to notice what they need. Trust that they can choose what serves them. And trust that, with guidance and patience, they can grow into digital citizens who are not ruled by devices, but who use them with clarity, intention, and integrity. This is not an abstract ideal—it is a practical, attainable goal. And it begins not with rules, but with relationships, reflection, and respect.

The Power of "Mindful Tech" – Using Digital Tools to Encourage Mindfulness Rather Than Distraction, and Real-World Strategies to Integrate Healthy Tech Habits

Technology's influence on the human mind is no longer theoretical—it is immediate, pervasive, and deeply personal. Children and teenagers, whose cognitive and emotional frameworks are still forming, are particularly vulnerable to the compulsive pull of apps designed to command attention and monetise engagement. Yet the same tools that fragment focus and feed distraction also contain the potential to cultivate calm, curiosity, and emotional clarity—*if* they are used with intention. This is the central promise of mindful tech: not to reject digital tools, but to transform their use from automatic compulsion to conscious choice.

Mindful tech begins with a shift in purpose. Whereas most apps and platforms are built around metrics like time-on-screen, shares, and clicks, mindful technology reorients the user's attention toward present-moment awareness, self-regulation, and psychological well-being. It includes everything from meditation apps and mood trackers to digital journals and guided breathing tools. But beyond the tools themselves, mindful tech is a philosophy—a way of relating to digital engagement that privileges reflection over reaction.

The term "mindfulness" often conjures images of silence, stillness, and solitude. While these qualities are important, they do not fully capture the relevance of mindfulness in the digital age. Here, mindfulness means awareness of how we *relate* to our technology—how it affects our emotions, thoughts, attention, and behaviours. For children and teens, developing this awareness is a foundational skill for digital resilience.

Consider the example of 13-year-old Aria, who struggled with anxiety and difficulty sleeping. Her evenings were filled with passive scrolling on social media, a habit that numbed her racing thoughts but left her restless and overstimulated. Her therapist introduced her to a simple mindfulness app that included body scans, breathing exercises, and journaling prompts. Aria began using it for just ten minutes before bed. Within weeks, she noticed a tangible difference—not only in her sleep quality but in her ability to notice emotional shifts during the day. What changed wasn't the amount of time she spent on screens, but *how* she spent it. Her device had become a support, not a stressor.

This transformation hinges on design as much as intention. Many mindfulness tools are explicitly built to support self-awareness. Headspace, Calm, and Insight Timer offer structured meditation programmes tailored for children and adolescents. Mood-tracking apps like Daylio or Moodnotes allow users to log emotional states and reflect on behavioural patterns. Gratitude journals, creative writing prompts, and focus timers (like Forest or Pomodoro-based tools) offer children a structured, calming digital experience, as opposed to the chaotic, fragmented nature of social media feeds.

But mindful tech does not require specialised apps to be effective. Any interaction with a device can be approached mindfully if guided by three questions: What am I using this for? How do I feel before and after? Is this aligned with my values and goals? These questions, when asked regularly, rewire the user's relationship with technology from reactive to reflective.

One powerful classroom-based initiative illustrates the impact of this practice. A middle school in Amsterdam introduced a "Digital Mindfulness Minute" at the beginning of every tech-based lesson. Before opening their devices, students were asked to pause, take a breath, and set an intention for their use. Whether it was to complete a writing assignment, research a topic, or connect with peers, the simple act of *naming* their purpose helped reduce impulsive tab-switching and increased task completion. Teachers reported improved focus and fewer disciplinary issues related to off-task digital behaviour. The intervention was minimal in terms of time but significant in its cognitive effect. It primed the brain for deliberate use rather than distraction.

At home, parents can cultivate mindful tech habits through collaborative dialogue and environmental design. One family in Singapore created a "mindful media nook"—a small, screen-equipped corner with soft lighting, headphones, and a set of agreed-upon apps for creative or calming use. This included drawing tools, piano tutorials, and a mindfulness app with visual breathing guides. By associating this space with intentional use, the family reframed screens from "default entertainment" to "purposeful engagement."

Equally important is *how* children transition *out* of screen use. Many digital meltdowns occur not because of screen exposure itself, but because of abrupt or emotionally dysregulated transitions. Mindful tech practices can help children close their devices with awareness, not agitation. For example, a "digital cool-down" routine—two minutes of reflective journaling, stretching, or breathwork after screen use—can help the brain reorient, regulate, and re-engage with the physical world.

There is also a growing case for using mindful tech to *retrain* attention. In a culture of constant multitasking, many children struggle with sustained focus. This is not a failure of willpower—it is a product of design. Apps and platforms bombard the brain with novelty, intermittent rewards, and social validation, training it to seek constant stimulation. Over time, this weakens the neural circuits responsible for sustained attention and impulse control. Mindfulness-based tech tools, particularly those that emphasise stillness, deep listening, or single-tasking, act as cognitive counterweights. They help rebuild the brain's capacity for focus—not by forcing it, but by gently encouraging it.

It is also worth exploring the social dimensions of mindful tech. Group meditations via video chat, collective gratitude journals, or shared silence practices can deepen a sense of connection, especially for teens navigating the performative pressures of digital life. These practices remind them that online interactions need not be performative or comparative—they can be grounded, reciprocal, and supportive.

Mindful tech is not a panacea. It cannot compensate for poor sleep, social isolation, or chronic stress. Nor can it replace the irreplaceable: time in nature, real-world relationships, and unstructured play. But it can serve as a bridge—a way to use the tools of the digital world to point children back to themselves. It offers a counter-narrative to the myth that tech must always be stimulating, fast, or addictive. Instead, it says: here is a way to *pause*, to *feel*, to *choose*.

The challenge, of course, is cultural. Most mainstream platforms are designed to fragment attention, not deepen it. Algorithms favour content that provokes rather than soothes, distracts rather than focuses. Teaching children to use mindful tech means helping them see this clearly. When they understand that their emotional state is not random, but influenced by design, they begin to reclaim agency. They start to ask, not just what they are consuming, but what it is *doing* to them.

This kind of awareness must be cultivated over time. Schools can integrate digital mindfulness into health curricula. Parents can model mindful tech use by narrating their choices aloud: "I'm setting a timer so I don't lose track of time," or "I'm choosing this app because it helps me unwind." These small acts of transparency create a culture in which intentionality is normalised.

Ultimately, the power of mindful tech lies not in its novelty, but in its *discipline.* It teaches children that technology is not merely a source of entertainment or information—it is a tool that can either cloud or clarify the mind. When used with care, digital tools can help children develop a sense of emotional granularity, sharpen their attention, and cultivate habits that support rather than sabotage their well-being.

In an age where every swipe is engineered for engagement, and every notification tugs at the mind's seams, mindfulness becomes a revolutionary act. Teaching children to engage with tech mindfully is not about controlling them—it is about equipping them. Equipping them to think before they click, to feel before they respond, and to choose presence in a world that constantly tempts distraction. This is the heart of mindful tech: not merely using screens with awareness, but living *with* awareness—online and off.

Emotional Intelligence in the Digital Age – How Constant Exposure to Online Interactions Affects Emotional Maturity, Empathy, and Real-World Relationships

Emotional intelligence—the capacity to recognise, understand, and manage our own emotions while empathising with the emotions of others—is not a static trait. It is a set of dynamic skills cultivated over time through meaningful human interaction. In the formative years of a child's life, these skills are primarily shaped in the context of face-to-face communication: eye contact, vocal tone, body language, and the subtle rhythms of conversation. However, in today's hyperconnected world, much of that interpersonal terrain has shifted online. Increasingly, children and teenagers are learning about relationships, conflict resolution, and emotional expression not in living rooms and classrooms, but through screens and devices. This shift raises critical questions: What is the impact of constant digital interaction on emotional development? How does it shape empathy, self-awareness, and social connection? And what can we do to ensure that emotional intelligence not only survives, but thrives, in the digital age?

At the heart of emotional intelligence is the ability to attune to others—to read the nuances of a friend's facial expression, to sense discomfort in a peer's silence, to notice the emotional undercurrents in a conversation. These skills are honed through repeated, real-world experiences where communication is messy, unpredictable, and richly textured. Digital communication, by contrast, flattens much of this complexity. Text messages strip away tone. Emojis compress feeling into symbols. Reactions—likes, hearts, fire emojis—replace thoughtful feedback. While these tools offer speed and convenience, they often short-circuit the processes through which emotional depth and social attunement are developed.

This does not mean that digital communication is inherently damaging. Rather, it requires conscious scaffolding. Without deliberate guidance, children may internalise a skewed understanding of emotion—one that privileges performativity over authenticity, immediacy over reflection, and curated personas over genuine vulnerability. These patterns, when reinforced over time, can dull the capacity for empathy, reduce tolerance for emotional discomfort, and hinder the ability to form and sustain deep relationships.

Consider the experience of sixteen-year-old Mira, whose friendships existed almost entirely through messaging apps and social media. While she appeared highly connected—maintaining dozens of chats daily—she struggled with anxiety and interpersonal conflict. When a misunderstanding arose with a close friend, Mira chose to ghost rather than resolve the issue directly. She later explained that she "didn't know how to handle it face-to-face" and feared the emotional intensity of a real conversation. Mira's avoidance was not a character flaw; it reflected a skill gap. She had never been taught how to read emotional cues in person or to navigate difficult dialogues. Her case is emblematic of a broader challenge: how digital fluency can coexist with emotional illiteracy.

Empathy, too, faces new pressures in a digital landscape. In traditional settings, empathy arises through shared experience and embodied interaction. A child sees a peer fall and winces instinctively. A teenager notices tension in a classmate's voice and responds with concern. These moments of felt resonance build emotional circuitry. Online, such cues are diminished or absent. When distress is conveyed through text or memes, it risks being minimised, misread, or ignored. Moreover, the design of many digital platforms—emphasising self-presentation, personal branding, and audience engagement—can shift attention inward. The more children are conditioned to view interactions through the lens of "How does this make me look?" rather than "How is the other person feeling?" the harder it becomes to develop empathy as a reflex.

This is especially true in environments that reward reactive behaviour. On social media, outrage spreads faster than compassion, and quick responses are often favoured over thoughtful reflection. When children engage in these dynamics without awareness, they may become emotionally desensitised, mistaking visibility for validation and mistaking agreement for understanding. Research from the University of Michigan found that college students' empathy scores had declined significantly over the past two decades, with the steepest drop occurring alongside the rise of social media. While correlation does not imply causation, the data underscore the need for deliberate cultivation of emotional intelligence in digitally saturated environments.

Yet digital platforms can also be harnessed to strengthen emotional intelligence—if used with intention. One powerful example comes from a secondary school in Dublin, which integrated digital storytelling into its emotional literacy curriculum. Students created short videos exploring personal challenges—bullying, anxiety, grief—and shared them within a secure classroom forum. The goal was not performance but connection. Classmates responded with supportive messages, reflecting on what they learned and how they felt. Over time, students reported increased empathy, deeper classroom cohesion, and greater comfort in discussing emotional topics. The digital medium became a bridge, not a barrier, precisely because it was framed around authenticity and reflection rather than performance and judgement.

Parents, too, play a critical role in shaping how children internalise emotional norms online. This starts with *modelling*: demonstrating how to engage thoughtfully, how to pause before responding to emotionally charged content, and how to bring emotional vocabulary into everyday conversation. When a parent comments, "That post made me feel really anxious—let's talk about why," they normalise emotional transparency. When they ask, "How do you think your friend felt when you didn't reply?" they prompt empathy. These micro-interventions build a culture of emotional curiosity and responsibility.

It is also vital to create spaces where children can practise emotional skills offline. Shared mealtimes, screen-free family activities, and unstructured play offer opportunities to read cues, negotiate conflict, and build rapport. Emotional intelligence does not develop in abstraction—it requires context. By balancing digital interaction with embodied connection, children learn to cross-translate between environments: to carry empathy from text to tone, to hold space for others beyond emojis, and to remain emotionally present even when screens are not.

Schools can extend this work by embedding social-emotional learning (SEL) into the digital citizenship curriculum. This means going beyond the usual topics of cyberbullying and privacy to explore how digital habits influence mood, how online personas differ from real-world identities, and how emotional boundaries can be honoured in virtual settings. Interactive modules that use role-play, journaling, and media analysis can help students reflect on their own emotional patterns and recognise the humanity behind the screen.

One promising strategy is the use of "empathy audits," where students periodically assess how their digital behaviour aligns with their emotional values. Are they listening or reacting? Are they seeking connection or validation? Are they showing up online as the friend they aspire to be? These questions, when posed with care and without moralism, support self-awareness and accountability.

We must also acknowledge that emotional development does not occur in a vacuum—it is shaped by culture, context, and power dynamics. Children from marginalised backgrounds may experience digital spaces as both a refuge and a threat. While online communities can offer validation and solidarity, they can also expose young people to discrimination, harassment, and misrepresentation. Emotional intelligence in the digital age must therefore include *critical* emotional literacy: the ability to recognise structural inequities, to name emotional labour, and to engage with difference ethically.

The stakes are high. Emotional intelligence is not a soft skill—it is a foundational capacity that underpins academic success, mental health, leadership, and civic engagement. In a world that increasingly mediates relationships through screens, we cannot leave emotional development to chance. We must actively design for it—through pedagogy, parenting, policy, and platform design.

This means advocating for tech that encourages nuance, not polarisation. It means creating environments—online and offline—where children can practise empathy, navigate disagreement, and express emotion without fear. It means honouring the full emotional spectrum, not just what is easy to post or like.

Ultimately, the question is not whether technology will shape our children's emotional lives—it already does. The real question is whether we will help them shape it back. Whether we will equip them with the tools to feel deeply, relate authentically, and respond wisely in a world that often rewards the opposite.

To raise emotionally intelligent children in the digital age is not to shield them from technology, but to teach them how to inhabit it with humanity. It is to remind them that behind every screen is a person—with fears, hopes, and complexity—and that every click, comment, and message is an opportunity to practise the most essential of human skills: empathy.

Creating Digital-Free Spaces at Home – The Importance of Setting Physical and Psychological Boundaries for Screen Use Without Making It Feel Like Punishment

In a culture of constant digital connection, where every space can be transformed into a portal for entertainment, information, and social interaction, the concept of a "digital-free zone" may feel antiquated or even adversarial. But creating such spaces in the home is not about imposing austerity; it is about reclaiming attention, presence, and the subtle rituals that sustain family life. Children today are not choosing between screens and no screens—they are growing up in a world where digital presence is ubiquitous, ambient, and often assumed. The challenge is not to extract them from this world, but to provide them with meaningful contrast: environments where the pace slows, the noise softens, and the mind is allowed to settle. Done thoughtfully, digital-free spaces are not punitive—they are restorative.

The value of digital-free zones lies in their symbolic and psychological significance. These are spaces where attention is no longer fragmented by notifications, where conversations are uninterrupted, and where solitude or connection can unfold without mediation. In a home without such spaces, children may never experience what it feels like to be fully present—with others, with their thoughts, or with their surroundings. Over time, this absence can dull emotional insight, impair concentration, and erode the capacity for deep relationships.

Establishing these spaces is not a matter of confiscating devices or enforcing strict rules, but of aligning physical design with family values. It is about sending a consistent message: that the home is not just a charging station or Wi-Fi hub, but a sanctuary for attention, reflection, and connection. This message is especially powerful when children are invited to co-create it. When digital boundaries are framed as shared commitments rather than unilateral mandates, they are more likely to be embraced—and even internalised.

Take the example of the D'Souza family in Bangalore, who were grappling with screen saturation during and after the COVID-19 lockdowns. With both parents working from home and two children attending school online, devices had invaded every room. The family felt fragmented—not just physically, but emotionally. Conversations were rushed or distracted. Meals were consumed in parallel with screens. Play had become background noise to digital consumption. Recognising the need for change, the family decided to make the dining area and living room digital-free zones. This decision was not presented as a punishment but as a family experiment: Could reclaiming these spaces improve their sense of connection?

To their surprise, the effect was almost immediate. Meals became more interactive. Arguments over screen time diminished, because the boundary was spatially clear and consistently respected. Most importantly, the children reported feeling "more noticed." This insight speaks volumes. In the absence of digital competition, attention regained its rightful place in the fabric of family life. The D'Souzas did not reduce screen time by decree; they reoriented it by design.

Psychologically, digital-free spaces help children delineate boundaries between different modes of being. Just as school uniforms or bedtime routines signal a shift in focus or energy, a digital-free space provides a cue that certain behaviours are expected here: conversation, reflection, rest, or creativity. This kind of spatial signalling is crucial for cognitive organisation. Without it, screens tend to bleed into every domain—turning bedrooms into entertainment zones, study desks into distraction centres, and family areas into multi-tasking battlegrounds. Boundaries restore intentionality.

Research supports this logic. A study published in *Pediatrics* found that children who used screens in their bedrooms were more likely to experience sleep disturbances, lower academic performance, and reduced physical activity. By contrast, households with clear screen-free zones—particularly during meals and before bed—reported better family cohesion and healthier sleep patterns. These effects are not merely behavioural; they are neurological. The brain needs context to regulate itself. Without physical boundaries, it struggles to shift between stimulation and stillness, focus and rest.

One common concern among parents is that establishing digital-free zones will provoke resistance, especially from older children and teenagers. This fear is not unfounded—but it is often overstated. When boundaries are introduced as part of a conversation about well-being, autonomy, and mutual respect, children are more receptive. The key is to avoid moralistic framing. Instead of saying, "You're addicted to your phone, so we're banning it from the living room," try, "We all need time and space to reconnect without distractions—let's choose a room where we can do that together." The difference in tone is crucial. One invites defensiveness; the other invites participation.

Moreover, digital-free spaces should not be spaces of deprivation. They should be enriched with alternatives that nourish attention and connection. Comfortable seating, books, music, games, art supplies, or simply the invitation to talk—all of these can help children see that what replaces screen time is not boredom, but something more textured and rewarding. Over time, these spaces become associated not with restriction, but with pleasure. The living room is where we laugh together. The dining table is where we share stories. The bedroom is where we unwind without the glow of a screen. These associations build habits—not just of behaviour, but of attention.

In households where space is limited, digital-free zones do not have to be grand or separate. A corner of a room, a designated time window, or even a shared agreement that certain activities remain screen-free can have the same effect. The goal is not architectural—it is relational. It is about carving out islands of presence in a sea of digital noise.

Digital-free spaces also serve as emotional safety zones. When conflict arises, they offer a place to decompress without retreating into digital distraction. When a child is upset, they can turn to a parent who is not simultaneously scrolling through messages. When a sibling wants to share something, they can trust that they have the other's attention. These micro-moments of attunement build trust, empathy, and emotional resilience. They teach children that presence matters—and that they are worthy of it.

Schools have begun to take note of this principle as well. Several forward-thinking institutions have introduced screen-free lounges, mindfulness rooms, or device-free play zones. The goal is not to eliminate technology from education but to balance it with opportunities for relational and sensory engagement. These models can inspire similar adaptations at home. Families might create weekend rituals around device-free mornings, or design evening routines that prioritise conversation over consumption. The specifics will vary—but the underlying message remains the same: Not every moment must be mediated by a screen.

Ultimately, creating digital-free spaces at home is not about controlling technology—it is about restoring context. It is about helping children feel the contrast between scattered attention and shared presence, between passive consumption and active engagement, between virtual connection and real-world intimacy. In doing so, we give them something that algorithms cannot provide: the experience of being fully seen, heard, and valued without distraction.

The task is not always easy. It requires consistency, creativity, and compassion. But the rewards are profound. In a world increasingly designed to fragment attention and commodify presence, the act of carving out space for what matters becomes an act of care. And in the quiet of those digital-free moments—over a meal, in a story, during a shared silence—children learn one of the most enduring lessons of all: that connection is not just about being online. It is about being *with*.

Interactive Exercise: The "Tech Detox Challenge" – A Structured Approach to Experimenting with Reduced Screen Time While Making It a Fun Family Activity

In a digitally saturated world, taking a step back from screens can feel both radical and restorative. The omnipresence of digital devices has quietly transformed the rhythm of family life—altering how we connect, communicate, and spend time together. While technology certainly brings convenience, connection, and entertainment, its unmoderated presence can also erode attention, diminish the quality of relationships, and crowd out essential moments of stillness and creativity. The "Tech Detox Challenge" was created not as a rule-bound restriction, but as a playful, reflective experiment to help families reconnect—with each other and with their own internal compass—by exploring life with less digital noise.

The concept of a "tech detox" often carries punitive connotations: a withdrawal, a cold-turkey rejection, a moral statement about excess. But reframed as a curiosity-driven family activity, it becomes something quite different. It becomes a shared exploration of what life feels like without the constant pull of notifications, algorithms, and infinite scroll. It is not about vilifying screens; it is about giving children—and adults—the chance to notice what happens in their absence.

The most successful tech detoxes are not dictated by top-down rules but are designed collaboratively. This collaborative spirit transforms the process from a chore into a challenge—something families embark on together, with each member contributing ideas, boundaries, and goals. The key to this approach is framing. Rather than asking, "How can we reduce screen time?" ask, "What would we like to make more space for?" This subtle shift helps children focus not on what is being taken away, but on what is being reclaimed: play, rest, conversation, imagination, presence.

Consider the experience of the Jaffar family in Kuala Lumpur, who took part in a one-week version of the Tech Detox Challenge. With two children aged eight and thirteen, they co-designed the structure together. Each family member nominated one non-digital activity they wished to prioritise. The younger child chose building a model village; the older opted to explore cooking. Their parents wanted more family meals and quiet evenings. Together, they decided to eliminate screens after 6 p.m. and to replace television with shared board games or music. They also made a shared commitment to spend part of each evening reflecting on how the detox was going—what was difficult, what felt different, and what they appreciated.

The first two days were, in their own words, "awkward and a little tense." Habitual routines were disrupted. The silence after dinner felt unfamiliar. The children initially complained of boredom. But by the third evening, a subtle shift had begun. The model village took shape. Meals extended into laughter. Evenings no longer ended in parallel scrolling but in shared conversation. By the end of the week, both children reported feeling "less rushed" and "more noticed." Most tellingly, they asked if the family could keep some version of the detox going. The Jaffars did not impose discipline—they facilitated *discovery*.

At its core, the Tech Detox Challenge is an invitation to conduct a social experiment—one rooted in observation, play, and gentle recalibration. It can be adapted in length and intensity. Some families begin with 24 hours; others stretch the process over weekends or select days of the week. Some set time-based boundaries—such as no devices after 7 p.m.—while others designate specific spaces as screen-free. What matters is not the structure itself, but the spirit in which it is undertaken: open, collaborative, and curious.

To be effective, the challenge must include regular reflection. Children are capable of deep insight when invited to explore their own behaviours without fear of judgement. Parents can prompt this reflection with open-ended questions: How did it feel not to check your phone this evening? What did you notice when the television wasn't on? What did we do together that we don't usually make time for? These questions are not meant to elicit "right" answers but to develop self-awareness—an essential foundation for long-term digital self-regulation.

Families often discover unexpected emotional layers during the detox. Some children may experience a sense of relief—the pressure to be constantly responsive, entertaining, or "on" is momentarily lifted. Others may confront discomfort: restlessness, anxiety, or the impulse to fill every quiet moment. These emotional responses are not signs of failure; they are evidence of what the detox reveals. The challenge surfaces what digital routines may be masking—boredom, fatigue, loneliness, or overstimulation—and offers a space to process these emotions together, rather than numbing them with devices.

It also allows for the rediscovery of analogue pleasures: the tactile satisfaction of drawing, the unhurried joy of board games, the intimacy of shared reading. These activities are not nostalgia—they are neural nourishment. They support attention span, creativity, emotional regulation, and interpersonal attunement in ways that digital engagement, for all its benefits, often does not. Reconnecting with these forms of play and rest provides children with a broader repertoire of self-soothing and self-expression—tools they can return to even after the challenge ends.

Importantly, the Tech Detox Challenge also serves as a mirror for adult behaviour. Children model what they see. If a parent insists on digital abstinence while checking work emails at the dinner table, the message becomes contradictory. But when adults participate fully—admitting their own habits, sharing their own challenges—the family dynamic shifts. Detoxing becomes a collective act of growth, not an imposed correction. It says: this is something we all wrestle with, and something we can support each other in improving.

Educators have also begun experimenting with similar models in schools. One secondary school in New Zealand piloted a "Digital Reflection Week," in which students agreed to limit personal device use and kept daily journals on their emotional, cognitive, and social experiences. The school reported increased engagement, more vibrant classroom discussions, and a notable drop in social conflict. While temporary, the exercise prompted lasting changes in student behaviour. Several pupils reported deleting apps or reorganising their home screens to reduce temptation. The lesson here is not about restriction—it's about *resetting the defaults*.

The Tech Detox Challenge can also extend beyond the home. Families can collaborate with extended relatives, friends, or neighbours to create community-based detox days or weekends. Group activities—nature walks, collective meals, storytelling circles—amplify the experience and reduce feelings of isolation. They remind children that digital reduction is not deprivation, but a form of social and emotional abundance.

Of course, the aim is not to demonise technology or to instil guilt around screen use. Children live in a world where screens are tools for learning, expression, and connection. But like all tools, they require thoughtful use. The Tech Detox Challenge helps develop the habit of discernment: the ability to pause and ask, "Is this helping or hindering me right now?" "Is this filling a need—or avoiding one?" These are not just questions about devices—they are questions about self-awareness, boundaries, and values.

After the challenge, families should reflect not only on what was difficult, but on what they want to carry forward. Perhaps a screen-free breakfast becomes a daily ritual. Perhaps a single evening a week remains device-free. Perhaps a new shared activity discovered during the detox becomes a lasting family tradition. The detox, then, becomes less of a break and more of a bridge—to healthier rhythms, clearer boundaries, and richer relationships.

In a culture that often equates stimulation with happiness and connectivity with value, the Tech Detox Challenge offers a gentle counterpoint. It invites families to explore slowness, to rediscover depth, and to cultivate attention as an act of care. It demonstrates that stepping away from screens is not about going backward—it's about *coming back*: to the body, to the moment, to each other. And in doing so, it offers children something rare and precious in the digital age—a felt sense of presence, undivided and real.

Chapter 5
The Social and Emotional Impact of Screen Culture

For today's children and adolescents, digital spaces don't merely complement their social lives—they *are* their social lives. Friendships take root in group chats, tensions simmer and spill over in comment threads, identities are sculpted through bios and profile pictures, and emotional states are expressed—often exaggerated—in the public metrics of likes, stories, and shares. These platforms offer remarkable avenues for self-expression, belonging, and creativity. But that's not the whole story. Alongside the promise of connection, there's a more troubling undercurrent: anxiety, alienation, comparison, and a relentless pressure to perform. In this chapter, we step into that contradiction—how digital culture builds bridges even as it sometimes builds walls, how it amplifies young voices while subtly distorting the way they come to see themselves.

Social media was built, ostensibly, to connect us. And for children—especially during the emotionally charged years of adolescence—it often delivers on that promise. The ability to maintain friendships outside school hours, to explore identities that may not feel safe or accepted offline, or to find one's people in far-flung corners of the internet can be not just affirming, but life-saving. This is especially true for young people who feel marginalised or misunderstood in their immediate environments. Digital spaces, at their best, can offer room to breathe.

Still, it's within those very spaces of connection that something quieter—and more troubling—can begin to unfold. The always-on nature of digital life creates the illusion of social saturation, yet many young people report a gnawing sense of emotional isolation. There's a strange contradiction here: being perpetually connected and yet feeling utterly alone. Why? In part, because so much of what plays out online is curated. The unspoken rule is that you show the best version of yourself—or at least the most interesting. Authenticity becomes a liability. Vulnerability, a risk. Popularity, meanwhile, is no longer just a social metric; it's an algorithmic one. Engagement drives visibility, and visibility often becomes a proxy for worth.

This system isn't simply the byproduct of user behaviour. It's built into the scaffolding of the platforms themselves. Algorithms prioritise what's engaging, clickable, shareable—not necessarily what's sincere or meaningful. And while children may not understand these mechanics consciously, they feel them. They adapt to them. They learn that attention is won by aesthetics, by volume, by speed—and that silence, on these platforms, can feel like erasure.

One of the most insidious consequences of this ecosystem is something researchers have started to name: *networked loneliness*. Despite the illusion of endless connection, many young people report feeling emotionally adrift. Data from the UK's Office for National Statistics suggests that children who spend more time on social media—particularly when that time is passive, spent scrolling rather than interacting—are more likely to feel lonely. There's a cruel irony here. The more they observe others engaging, the more acutely they feel their own exclusion. The party they didn't attend. The inside joke they weren't part of. The message thread that's gone quiet. Each scroll delivers a fresh reminder of what they're missing, even when nothing has actually changed.

It's not that social media directly *causes* loneliness. But it undoubtedly reframes the experience of being young and socially aware. Comparison, once confined to the occasional awkward school corridor or family function, is now ambient. Omnipresent. A peer's popularity, beauty, or achievements aren't just known—they're on display, often relentlessly. These micro-moments accumulate. Quietly. Perpetually. They erode self-confidence in ways that are hard to name, let alone reverse.

Then there's digital peer pressure—a force as old as adolescence itself, now intensified by the speed and scope of the online world. Where peer influence once came from the friend group, the classroom, the neighbourhood, it now flows from countless sources: influencers, viral trends, aesthetic templates. The norms are often unspoken but heavily enforced. Participate, or disappear. Conform, or risk exclusion. And because the pace of digital culture is relentless, there's little room to pause and ask, "Do I even want to do this?"

Twelve-year-old Ayaan put it plainly in a school workshop: he felt he *had* to join every TikTok trend, not out of joy, but out of fear. "If you're not in it," he said, "you're not in the group chat anymore." His screen time skyrocketed, not from enjoyment, but from a kind of anxious necessity. It's easy, from the outside, to misread this as frivolous. But what often looks like aimless scrolling is, for many children, a form of social currency management. A survival tactic, in a space where attention is everything.

Naturally, this begins to shape how children view themselves. The feedback loops of social media—likes, shares, reposts—train young users to seek affirmation externally. A well-received photo boosts confidence, but also sets a standard. Now the next post must perform equally well—or better. The absence of engagement can feel like disapproval, even invisibility. Before long, children stop asking "What do I think of this?" and begin asking, reflexively, "Will it get likes?" Identity, once rooted in inner values, becomes a performance for an imagined audience.

Parents often struggle to intervene—not for lack of concern, but because they're working against design. Social platforms are engineered to be compelling, to draw users back in, again and again. Yet, there are openings. Gentle ones. Encouraging children to notice how they feel before and after social media use—energised? depleted? anxious?—can plant seeds of awareness. Helping them create posts that reflect their interests rather than aim to impress can subtly shift the relationship. And modelling healthy disengagement—showing that one's self-worth isn't tied to metrics—can speak louder than any lecture.

Cyberbullying deserves its own lens here, not just as an issue of cruelty, but of context. It's not always overt abuse. Often, it's the subtler wounds: exclusion from a group chat, the cold sting of ghosting, the sting of a sarcastic comment masked as a joke. These forms of harm are harder to detect, and easier to dismiss. But for the child on the receiving end, the impact is real. When conflict plays out in public threads or is captured in screenshots, the sense of exposure can be deeply shaming. The digital leaves fewer places to hide—and no room to forget.

True resilience in this arena isn't built on fear-based warnings. It's built on *relational literacy*—the ability to read emotional cues, navigate disagreement, and ask for help when needed. It also requires adult presence that is not reactionary, but responsive. When children sense that they can talk about their online world without being punished, dismissed, or pathologised, they are more likely to open up. Emotional safety is the foundation. From there, resilience can take root.

This chapter also creates space for stories—real ones—from young people who have met these challenges with courage, and found new paths through them. There's Sara, 15, who stepped away from Instagram for three months after realising how much it was distorting her self-image. In that time, she reconnected with drawing and began showing her work in local galleries. Or Dev, 14, who started a school podcast on digital ethics, inviting classmates to talk honestly about their screen habits, fears, and small victories. These aren't stories of abstinence, but of agency. They remind us what becomes possible when children are given the room—and the trust—to reflect and reorient.

The emotional weight of growing up online isn't always visible. It shows up in small gestures: the pause before speaking, the anxiety of being overlooked, the tiredness of always performing. It's in the ache of comparison, the jolt of digital praise, the quiet shame of exclusion. But within this tangled web lies a rare opportunity—to help children not just *survive* their digital lives, but inhabit them more fully, more wisely, more humanely.

In the pages ahead, we'll delve further into these tensions and explore what they mean for relationships, identity, and emotional growth. Not to cast technology as villain or saviour, but to remind ourselves: behind every post, every avatar, every device-holding hand, is a child trying to make sense of a world that feels both astonishingly connected and bewilderingly complex. And in that effort, they are looking—urgently, silently, hopefully—to us. For guidance. For listening ears. For reassurance that their value isn't up for measurement. That it lies, always, in who they are—not in how many people click to see.

From Connection to Isolation – The Social Paradox of Technology

Social media platforms have, in a remarkably short span of time, redefined the architecture of childhood and adolescence. Once relegated to face-to-face encounters and telephone calls, young people's social lives now unfold predominantly through digital intermediaries—Snapchat streaks, WhatsApp groups, Instagram stories, gaming chats, and TikTok comment threads. These platforms promise connection, and in many ways they deliver it. Children can keep in touch with peers across time zones, discover communities that reflect their interests or identities, and find comfort in knowing they are not alone in their experiences. Yet, paradoxically, this perpetual connectivity often leads to a profound sense of disconnection. The more "connected" children become, the more susceptible they may be to feelings of exclusion, comparison, and loneliness. This is the social paradox of technology—one that parents and educators must urgently unpack with nuance and care.

The contradiction is best understood by examining the psychological nature of connection itself. Human beings are wired for belonging, but not merely in terms of presence. True connection involves emotional reciprocity, embodied cues, and sustained attention—elements that are often missing or muted in digital interaction. A "like" on a photo may signal affirmation, but it does not convey the depth of a meaningful glance or a listening ear. A heart emoji can stand in for care, yet it cannot offer the warmth of real companionship. Over time, these surface-level interactions, while abundant, can begin to feel hollow. The child receiving hundreds of likes may still feel unseen; the teen with constant notifications may still feel alone.

This experience of *networked loneliness* is increasingly documented in psychological research. A 2023 study conducted by the University of Bath found that adolescents who spent more than three hours a day on social media were significantly more likely to report feelings of isolation—particularly when their usage was passive in nature. That is, scrolling through others' posts, observing interactions without participating, or silently comparing themselves to curated depictions of peers. These findings echo earlier research from the University of Pennsylvania, which demonstrated that reducing social media use to 30 minutes a day led to measurable improvements in well-being, including reductions in loneliness and depression. What this body of work suggests is not that social media is inherently harmful, but that the *quality* of online engagement is what truly matters.

Children, particularly those navigating the emotionally fraught landscape of adolescence, are exquisitely sensitive to social cues. In digital spaces, those cues are not only reduced but algorithmically filtered. What they see, and what they are seen for, is shaped by design systems optimised not for authentic connection, but for engagement metrics. A child's visibility is tethered to performative success—their ability to post compelling content, to respond quickly, to maintain digital "presence." This creates a subtle but persistent anxiety: Am I being seen? Am I being responded to? Am I being excluded? The absence of a reply or a missed tag can carry an emotional weight disproportionate to its offline equivalent, precisely because it is interpreted through the lens of this persistent visibility.

Consider thirteen-year-old Mia, whose parents noticed a marked change in her mood after she joined a popular social media platform. Although she was more "social" than ever—constantly messaging friends, posting updates, and engaging in online banter—she began expressing feelings of being left out. As it turned out, she had become fixated on observing her friends' interactions without always participating. Photos from group outings she wasn't invited to, inside jokes in comments she didn't understand, or simply the absence of likes on her own posts created a silent narrative of rejection. Her parents, initially confused by the apparent contradiction between her social engagement and her growing sadness, came to understand that *digital presence is not the same as emotional inclusion.*

The paradox is further complicated by the nature of digital friendships. Many children maintain large networks of peers online, but these relationships are often shallow or transactional. The boundaries of friendship blur when connection is reduced to quick replies, memes, or comment exchanges. While there is nothing inherently wrong with these forms of contact, they rarely allow for the depth of sharing or vulnerability required to feel truly known. For children already struggling with social confidence, this environment can exacerbate insecurity. The safety of screens can become a hiding place from the risk of rejection—but it also becomes a barrier to real connection.

Parents seeking to support their children through this paradox face a delicate challenge. It is tempting to respond with restriction—to limit social media use, confiscate phones, or declare "digital detoxes." And in some cases, especially when emotional distress is acute, this may be warranted. But without deeper engagement, these actions can feel punitive or disconnected from the child's lived experience. The key lies in *curiosity and co-regulation*. Rather than approaching digital social life as a problem to be fixed, parents can approach it as a *world to be explored*—together with their children.

Open-ended dialogue is essential. Asking questions like, "How do you feel when you're scrolling through your feed?" or "Have you ever felt left out online?" invites children into reflective space without shame or defensiveness. Parents can share their own experiences—whether with digital fatigue, comparison, or emotional disconnection—to normalise these feelings and model vulnerability. The goal is to create a climate where children can name their experiences honestly, without fearing judgement or overreaction.

It is also helpful to support children in developing a nuanced vocabulary around digital connection. Terms like *ambient connection* (being aware of others without interacting), *FOMO* (fear of missing out), and *parasocial relationships* (one-sided relationships with influencers or online personas) can empower children to articulate experiences they may not have had words for. When children understand that their emotional responses are not failures but reflections of structural dynamics, they are more likely to feel agency in how they engage.

One powerful intervention is helping children differentiate between *connection* and *contact.* Contact refers to the frequency or volume of interactions; connection refers to their depth and meaning. Encouraging children to invest in fewer, more intentional relationships—even online—can shift the emphasis from performance to presence. Supporting them in creating smaller group chats for deeper conversation, taking breaks from platforms that foster comparison, or engaging in shared creative projects online (such as collaborative storytelling or music) can enhance the quality of digital interaction.

Equally important is ensuring that digital connections are *balanced* by embodied ones. The power of real-world interaction cannot be overstated. The subtle feedback loops of eye contact, tone of voice, shared laughter, or silent presence provide children with the emotional data they need to build empathy, self-awareness, and resilience. Families that prioritise device-free rituals—meals, walks, creative play—create microenvironments where these cues are preserved and celebrated. Schools, too, can play a vital role by fostering group work, discussion-based learning, and digital literacy programmes that centre emotional intelligence.

The social paradox of technology is not an indictment of digital culture. It is an invitation to reimagine it. Children do not need less connection—they need *deeper* connection. They need adults who understand that online life is not trivial but formative. They need spaces where digital performance is not the price of inclusion. And they need tools to distinguish between being visible and being valued.

The task ahead is not to eliminate the digital world from childhood, but to infuse it with *humanity.* To help children recognise when connection becomes comparison, when attention becomes anxiety, and when presence is being replaced by performance. In doing so, we prepare them not just to survive the complexities of online life, but to shape it—with empathy, with awareness, and with a sense of belonging that is not measured in metrics, but felt in the quiet, sustaining rhythms of real relationship.

Digital Peer Pressure and Online Trends – Why Viral Challenges, Influencer Culture, and Digital "Fitting In" Can Be as Powerful as Real-World Peer Influence

Peer pressure has long been recognised as a powerful force in childhood and adolescence—a developmental pressure point where the desire to belong can override personal judgement. In the digital age, this influence has not diminished; it has simply evolved. The corridors of peer influence have shifted from playgrounds and classrooms to social feeds and algorithmic platforms, where approval is quantified and visibility equates to social currency. Viral challenges, influencer endorsements, aesthetic trends, and digital norms now form an ecosystem where conformity is public, immediate, and relentlessly reinforced. The result is a kind of social theatre in which children not only perform their identities but are rewarded—or penalised—according to how well they align with prevailing digital scripts.

Unlike traditional peer pressure, which is often confined to specific social groups or physical settings, digital peer pressure operates on a broader, more insidious scale. It is ambient, ever-present, and amplified by the reach of social media. The child who once compared themselves to a handful of classmates now compares themselves to hundreds—sometimes thousands—of peers, influencers, and anonymous trendsetters. These comparisons are not theoretical; they are encoded in metrics: likes, shares, views, and followers. Every post becomes a potential test of acceptance, and every silence, a potential sign of exclusion.

This dynamic is particularly potent in the context of viral challenges. From dance routines and comedic skits to more controversial stunts, these challenges thrive on replication. Their very structure invites participation: mimic the behaviour, post the result, and await social approval. On the surface, many of these trends seem innocuous—an opportunity for fun, creativity, or shared experience. But they also create a powerful behavioural script: if you do this, you belong; if you don't, you're invisible. The fear of missing out becomes not just emotional but existential. For some children, the pressure to participate can override personal discomfort or ethical hesitation. They may attempt physically risky stunts, repeat inappropriate jokes, or parody behaviours they don't understand—all in service of being seen.

Take, for example, the case of a twelve-year-old girl in Delhi who participated in a popular but dangerous challenge involving the consumption of excessive quantities of spicy food. Although she disliked spicy food and later suffered severe digestive distress, she admitted to joining in because "everyone else had already posted their videos." Her admission revealed the deeper force at play: the challenge was not about enjoyment—it was about *social positioning*. To abstain would have meant exclusion; to participate, however unpleasant, was to be visible.

Influencer culture further complicates this terrain. Influencers, especially micro-influencers and teen content creators, often serve as aspirational figures—projecting curated lifestyles that blend authenticity with performance. Children and adolescents, still forming their identities, are especially susceptible to internalising these projections. They emulate clothing styles, speech patterns, beauty standards, and consumption habits not merely as a form of admiration, but as a means of aligning with perceived norms. This alignment is not passive—it is strategic. Children quickly learn that mimicking popular digital archetypes can increase their own social capital, while divergence can invite ridicule or invisibility.

The psychological effects of this constant mirroring are profound. Over time, children may begin to suppress aspects of their personality that do not align with dominant digital narratives. A child who enjoys classical music may downplay their interest in favour of more "trendy" genres. A teen who values privacy may feel compelled to overshare for fear of seeming aloof. This erosion of authenticity can lead to chronic self-monitoring, anxiety, and emotional dissonance. What was once internal self-esteem becomes externalised, contingent on maintaining a digital persona that garners approval.

Moreover, digital peer pressure is not limited to content creation. It extends to *consumption* as well. Children are acutely aware of what their peers are watching, listening to, or commenting on. To not engage with a viral series, a trending audio clip, or a controversial post is to risk being excluded from conversations. This creates a compulsive loop where engagement is driven less by interest and more by a fear of being left behind. For neurodivergent children, or those who struggle with social communication, this pressure can be particularly overwhelming. The demand to stay culturally current, digitally fluent, and socially responsive becomes a constant source of stress.

Parents often feel ill-equipped to counter this force. Traditional strategies—limiting screen time, discouraging specific apps, or banning trends—can backfire if implemented without understanding. Children may interpret these efforts as punitive or out of touch, reinforcing secrecy or shame. What is needed instead is a deeper engagement with the *social logic* of online trends. Rather than asking, "Why are you wasting time on this?" parents might ask, "What do you like about this trend? How does it make you feel when you post or when others respond?" These questions open a channel for reflection rather than resistance.

One powerful strategy is helping children build a critical lens. Media literacy programmes that dissect the mechanics of virality, the economic incentives behind influencer culture, and the psychological design of apps can be transformative. When children understand that trends are often engineered to maximise engagement—not meaning—they begin to see participation as a choice rather than a requirement. They learn to ask: Is this something I *want* to do, or something I *feel expected* to do?

Educators can also play a pivotal role. By integrating digital ethics into the classroom—not as a warning, but as an inquiry—teachers can help students navigate online norms with more confidence and autonomy. Role-playing exercises, group discussions, and analysis of real-life case studies allow children to explore scenarios without judgment. For instance, examining a viral trend's origin, evolution, and ethical implications can help students understand how trends spread and what consequences they might entail—social, emotional, or even legal.

Crucially, we must move beyond the binary of "good" and "bad" screen use. Not all digital trends are harmful. Many foster creativity, humour, solidarity, or activism. The #BlackLivesMatter movement, climate action campaigns, and mental health awareness challenges have shown how digital peer influence can be harnessed for social good. The key is helping children discern when they are acting out of agency and when they are reacting out of pressure. This discernment is a cornerstone of digital resilience.

Families can support this discernment by creating space for *offline belonging*. When children experience meaningful connection at home—in conversation, play, shared rituals—they become less reliant on digital performance for validation. When they feel seen and valued without needing to post, they are better equipped to resist the more corrosive aspects of peer pressure. And when they know that missteps can be discussed openly, without shame, they are more likely to seek help when online pressures become overwhelming.

Ultimately, digital peer pressure is not about technology alone—it is about *belonging*. It is about children's fundamental need to feel included, respected, and affirmed. The platforms that mediate this need are evolving rapidly, but the underlying psychology remains constant. What changes is how we, as adults, respond. We can choose to pathologise children's digital behaviour, or we can choose to understand it. We can impose rules from above, or we can co-create values from within. When we choose the latter, we empower children not just to navigate online culture, but to shape it—intelligently, ethically, and in alignment with who they really are.

Digital peer pressure, in all its complexity, reflects a truth that has always defined childhood: that fitting in matters. Our role is not to deny this truth, but to expand its boundaries—so that children can fit in without losing themselves. And perhaps even, in time, find the courage to stand out.

Social Media and Self-Worth – Breaking the Validation Loop

The metrics of childhood have changed. Where once affirmation came from a smile, a word of encouragement, or a shared glance, it now often arrives in the form of likes, shares, views, and follower counts. These digital tokens, while superficially innocuous, have quietly embedded themselves into the psychology of young users, reshaping how self-worth is constructed, measured, and pursued. For children and adolescents growing up immersed in social media, the feedback mechanisms of these platforms can be both addictive and defining. Understanding how this validation loop operates—and how to disrupt it—is one of the most pressing challenges facing parents, educators, and caregivers in the digital age.

At the core of the validation loop is the brain's reward circuitry. Social media platforms are engineered to exploit the same neurological pathways triggered by gambling, sugar, and other forms of behavioural reinforcement. When a child receives a like or a positive comment, the brain releases a small burst of dopamine—a neurotransmitter associated with pleasure and motivation. This creates a feedback loop: the behaviour (posting content) leads to reward (digital affirmation), which reinforces the behaviour. Over time, the brain begins to anticipate the reward, driving the child to seek it out repeatedly. What may begin as a casual interaction with peers can quickly escalate into a dependency on external validation for emotional regulation.

The process is especially potent during adolescence—a developmental stage characterised by heightened sensitivity to social evaluation. Brain imaging studies, such as those conducted at UCLA's Ahmanson-Lovelace Brain Mapping Center, have shown that the reward centres of adolescent brains are significantly more active than those of adults when receiving social approval online. This heightened reactivity means that digital affirmation does not merely feel good—it *matters*, sometimes profoundly. A post that garners widespread engagement can uplift mood and enhance self-confidence; one that goes unnoticed can provoke self-doubt, anxiety, or shame.

Crucially, the validation loop is not limited to active posting. It extends to the *anticipation* of reaction and the *comparison* with others. Children do not merely evaluate their worth based on their own metrics—they evaluate it in relation to their peers. How many likes did they get? Who commented? Was it shared? Did someone they admire repost it? This comparative logic transforms social interaction into a silent competition, one that rewards popularity over authenticity and visibility over depth. In such an environment, the pressure to curate an idealised digital self becomes overwhelming.

Consider fourteen-year-old Nia, who described spending over an hour editing each photo she posted, carefully selecting filters, crafting captions, and timing uploads to maximise engagement. When one post received fewer likes than usual, she deleted it within minutes. "It just felt like no one cared," she said. Her experience is not uncommon. Many teenagers describe linking their self-worth to the performance of their posts, interpreting each engagement metric as a referendum on their value. This reliance on digital affirmation can undermine intrinsic self-esteem—the stable sense of worth that arises from personal values, effort, and relationships—replacing it with a volatile, externally dependent form of self-regard.

What makes this dynamic especially troubling is its invisibility. Unlike overt bullying or harassment, the psychological harm of the validation loop often goes unrecognised. Children may not articulate their distress, and parents may struggle to detect it. After all, they are "just using social media"—interacting, sharing, connecting. But beneath this surface lies a subtle form of emotional conditioning, one that teaches children to conflate attention with affection, engagement with esteem.

Breaking this loop requires a multi-layered approach—one that addresses both the psychological mechanics of validation and the cultural narratives that sustain them. First, children must be supported in developing *awareness*. They need to recognise how platforms are designed to keep them engaged, how algorithms amplify certain behaviours, and how metrics are used to shape their attention. This kind of media literacy is not about fear—it is about empowerment. When children understand that the system is engineered to provoke certain responses, they are better positioned to observe their own reactions with curiosity rather than compulsion.

Second, it is essential to reorient children's focus from *performance* to *expression*. When the purpose of posting shifts from seeking approval to sharing meaning, the psychological stakes diminish. Parents can support this by praising creativity, authenticity, and effort, rather than popularity. A child who posts an original drawing or shares a thoughtful reflection deserves affirmation not because it was liked by hundreds, but because it represents something real. Reinforcing this message consistently—both online and offline—helps children internalise a sense of worth that is not tied to audience response.

Third, conversations about self-worth must be normalised. Children need to hear, explicitly and often, that their value is not contingent on how they are perceived. This means creating spaces where they can speak about insecurity without fear of ridicule, where disappointment over digital engagement can be met with empathy, and where alternative sources of self-esteem are cultivated. These include mastery (building skills), contribution (helping others), connection (being known and accepted), and identity (aligning with values). When these pillars are strong, the lure of superficial validation weakens.

Practical steps can support this psychological foundation. Encouraging regular digital pauses, where children step back from online platforms and engage in activities that offer intrinsic satisfaction, can help recalibrate their emotional baseline. Shared screen-free rituals—walks, creative projects, board games, or cooking—restore attention and rebuild relational depth. For older children, journaling about digital experiences can deepen self-awareness. Questions like "How did I feel before I posted this?" or "What did I hope to get from that comment?" can gently uncover motivations and patterns.

Schools also have a critical role to play. By integrating discussions of digital identity and emotional literacy into the curriculum, educators can foster reflective habits. Group dialogues about social media experiences—both positive and negative—can de-normalise the pursuit of validation and validate the full range of emotional responses. When children realise that others feel the same pressure, the shame of inadequacy begins to loosen. Collective reflection becomes a powerful antidote to the isolating effects of individual comparison.

Importantly, we must resist the urge to romanticise a pre-digital past or to cast technology as the villain. Social media, like all tools, is shaped by how it is used and understood. There are children who use platforms to advocate for justice, build community, express creativity, and deepen friendships. The aim is not to demonise social media, but to *humanise* its use—to help children remain grounded in their inherent worth even as they participate in online culture.

The validation loop can be broken—not through prohibition, but through *reconnection.* Reconnection to inner values, to meaningful relationships, and to experiences that affirm worth independently of reaction. It requires that we as adults model this ourselves: that we resist the lure of external metrics, that we speak honestly about our own digital habits, and that we show children what it looks like to live from the inside out.

Ultimately, teaching children to disentangle self-worth from social media is not just a digital literacy challenge—it is a developmental necessity. It is about protecting the core of who they are from the volatility of online performance. And it is about reminding them, again and again, that they are not a brand, a number, or a persona. They are a person—worthy, whole, and enough, exactly as they are.

Cyberbullying and Digital Conflicts – Recognising Subtle Forms of Online Aggression and Empowering Kids to Handle Negative Digital Interactions Effectively

In the digital age, conflict is no longer confined to playgrounds, classrooms, or whispered conversations behind closed doors. It follows children into their bedrooms, infiltrates their devices, and lingers long after school hours. Cyberbullying has emerged as one of the most pervasive threats to children's psychological well-being, not only because of its intensity, but because of its *invisibility*. It often wears a subtle cloak—quiet exclusions, passive-aggressive comments, insidious rumours, and veiled sarcasm, all delivered through platforms that blur the boundaries between public and private, joke and humiliation, real and performative. Understanding this complexity is essential for any adult seeking to protect and empower children in an era where conflict is algorithmically amplified and persistently archived.

Cyberbullying is commonly misunderstood as overt and aggressive—threats, name-calling, or public humiliation. But more often, it takes subtler forms that are no less harmful. A child being systematically left out of group chats, tagged in embarrassing photos, unfollowed en masse after a disagreement, or made the subject of sarcastic memes might struggle to articulate what's happening. Unlike traditional bullying, where power imbalances are often visible, digital aggression is laced with plausible deniability. "I was just joking," "It was only a meme," or "You're being too sensitive" are common refrains. These interactions may be dismissed as harmless, yet their cumulative psychological toll can be profound—eroding a child's sense of belonging, self-worth, and trust.

This erosion often occurs silently. A child may not report what they're experiencing because they fear it will be trivialised, or worse, result in further isolation. They may worry that adults won't understand the social dynamics at play, or that their access to devices will be restricted if they speak up. As a result, many endure digital hostility in silence—internalising the pain and often blaming themselves for their social discomfort.

Real-world examples illustrate the diverse manifestations of this phenomenon. In one widely discussed case, a 13-year-old student in a UK secondary school was gradually phased out of her peer group's online presence. They stopped tagging her in posts, removed her from shared playlists, and created parallel group chats to plan events without her. There were no explicit insults—just a slow, calculated withdrawal of visibility and inclusion. When she tried to confront the group, their response was dismissive: "We didn't think you were into it anymore." The girl, experiencing confusion and rejection, began to struggle with anxiety and school avoidance. Her parents only became aware of the issue months later when she broke down after seeing a group holiday photo online from which she had been deliberately excluded.

What makes digital conflict particularly difficult for children is its *persistence*. Unlike offline disputes that may fade with time, cyberbullying is often recorded, screenshotted, or left to circulate indefinitely. A hurtful comment or embarrassing photo can be revisited, relived, and re-shared—deepening emotional wounds with each encounter. This creates an emotional trap: the child feels both helpless to stop the aggression and unable to escape its consequences.

Empowering children to navigate this landscape begins with *recognition*. They must be taught that not all hurtful online behaviour looks like traditional bullying. Sarcasm, exclusion, digital ghosting, or even the strategic use of "likes" can all be used to assert dominance or inflict harm. Helping children understand *intent and impact*—that even seemingly minor acts can carry emotional weight—is key to building emotional literacy and self-trust.

Parents and educators must create environments where children feel safe discussing digital discomfort without fear of judgement or punishment. This requires active listening and a willingness to treat online interactions with the same seriousness as offline behaviour. When a child reports being excluded or mocked online, the adult response should not minimise their experience or dismiss it as "drama." Instead, it should validate their feelings, explore the context, and work collaboratively to address both the emotional and relational dimensions of the issue.

One practical approach is teaching children how to identify the emotional cues that signal digital distress. Do they feel anxious when checking their phone? Are they obsessively re-reading a comment thread? Do they hesitate to post out of fear? These bodily and emotional signals are often more reliable than the content itself. Helping children name these feelings, journal their experiences, or speak with a trusted adult can build the internal tools necessary for resilience.

Equally important is equipping children with proactive strategies to manage digital conflict. These include boundary-setting (such as muting or blocking toxic accounts), assertive communication ("I didn't find that funny, and I'd appreciate if you didn't post about me"), and knowing when to disengage. Role-playing difficult scenarios—such as how to respond to a hurtful comment or what to do when witnessing cyberbullying—can build confidence and preparedness.

It is also crucial to empower *bystanders*. Research consistently shows that peer intervention is one of the most effective deterrents to cyberbullying. Children who witness digital aggression but remain silent may do so out of uncertainty or fear. When schools and families normalise speaking up—whether by privately supporting a peer, reporting harmful content, or challenging toxic humour—they foster a culture where empathy is active, not passive. This sense of shared responsibility can dramatically shift the dynamics of online spaces.

The role of schools cannot be overstated. Digital citizenship education must go beyond privacy and password safety. It must delve into relational dynamics, ethical responsibility, and emotional impact. Schools should establish clear policies around online conduct, provide training for staff to recognise signs of cyberbullying, and create channels through which students can report digital conflict anonymously and safely. But policy alone is not enough; culture matters. Schools must foster environments where kindness is modelled, emotional intelligence is valued, and technology is used to uplift rather than demean.

Technology companies also have a role to play. The platforms that dominate young people's lives are not neutral. Their design choices—what gets prioritised in feeds, how content is moderated, which behaviours are rewarded—shape the social norms of digital interaction. Advocating for features that allow users to manage visibility, control comment settings, or flag subtle harassment can help rebalance the power dynamics in digital spaces. Parents and educators should encourage children to reflect critically on the platforms they use and to advocate for safer, more inclusive digital design.

Finally, children need models of repair. Conflict, digital or otherwise, is inevitable. What matters is not just how to avoid harm, but how to respond when it happens—whether as a victim, a bystander, or even a perpetrator. Teaching children how to apologise meaningfully, rebuild trust, or exit harmful dynamics with dignity gives them tools that will serve them for life. It reinforces the message that one's digital behaviour is not an abstract projection, but a reflection of real values and relationships.

Cyberbullying and digital conflict challenge us to rethink how we support children in their social development. The digital world is not a parallel universe—it is an extension of their emotional reality. When we help children understand this, when we validate their digital experiences, and when we equip them with language, strategies, and support, we do more than protect them from harm. We empower them to shape a digital culture rooted in empathy, respect, and authenticity. And that, in an age where aggression too often hides behind a screen, is an act of profound care.

Case Study: Real Stories of Kids Overcoming Social Media Struggles – Inspiring Accounts of Young People Who Learned to Balance Their Online Presence with Their Well-Being

In a world where digital identity is often conflated with personal identity, the pressure on children and adolescents to perform, conform, and engage on social media is immense. For many, the line between self-expression and self-surveillance becomes blurred. Likes and shares become proxies for approval, and visibility morphs into a marker of value. Yet amidst this landscape, there are compelling, instructive stories—narratives of young people who have consciously stepped back, re-evaluated their digital lives, and redefined their relationship with social media in ways that prioritise mental clarity, authenticity, and emotional well-being. These stories are neither naïve departures from the digital world nor dramatic rejections of technology. Rather, they exemplify a mature recalibration: a recognition that online life must be lived with boundaries, awareness, and intentionality.

Consider the case of Jaya, a fifteen-year-old student from Bangalore, who began using Instagram at the age of twelve. Initially drawn in by the creative potential of photography and filters, her account quickly evolved into a carefully curated performance of her daily life. By age fourteen, Jaya was posting almost daily, meticulously editing each image and strategising the optimal time to publish for maximum engagement. Her self-esteem became increasingly tied to the number of likes her posts received. On days when engagement was high, she felt energised and connected. On days when it fell short, she spiralled into self-doubt.

What ultimately prompted change was not an intervention from adults, but an introspective shift sparked by burnout. During exam season, Jaya attempted a self-imposed social media break to focus on studying. What she discovered surprised her: she slept better, felt less anxious, and began noticing how much mental energy had previously been devoted to maintaining her digital presence. Encouraged by this clarity, she extended her break and used the time to journal her thoughts on self-worth and identity. She later returned to Instagram with a markedly different approach—posting less frequently, disabling visible like counts, and using the platform primarily to follow artists and educational accounts rather than peers. Jaya's transformation did not come from external restriction but from *internal reflection*—an awakening to the cost of constant online performance.

Then there is Luca, a thirteen-year-old in Manchester, who found himself enmeshed in group chat dynamics that oscillated between camaraderie and cruelty. The group, composed of classmates, was active nearly every hour of the day. At first, the nonstop messaging felt exhilarating—a sense of inclusion, a digital playground. But it soon became toxic. Passive-aggressive comments, silent exclusions, and covert screenshots turned the chat into a minefield. Luca began experiencing symptoms of chronic stress: irritability, stomach aches, reluctance to go to school. Yet he struggled to name the source of his discomfort, as nothing within the group was overtly abusive. It was the *tone*, the context, the relentless scrutiny that weighed on him.

With the help of a school counsellor, Luca began mapping the emotional texture of his digital interactions. He kept a simple log of how he felt before and after engaging with the group chat. Over several weeks, patterns emerged: he consistently felt worse after participating, particularly during late evening hours. Equipped with this insight, he chose to leave the group—a decision that initially triggered backlash but ultimately led to relief. In the months that followed, Luca shifted his social energy to offline friendships rooted in shared interests rather than constant contact. He also joined a moderated online forum for young musicians, where he felt safer expressing himself without fear of social punishment. His story is a testament to the importance of emotional attunement and the power of supportive adults in helping children name and navigate subtle forms of digital harm.

A different kind of story emerges from Zara, a seventeen-year-old in Toronto, whose relationship with social media was shaped by activism. As a vocal advocate for climate justice, Zara used Twitter and TikTok to amplify awareness and mobilise peers. Her posts often went viral, drawing praise but also vitriolic backlash. While she felt empowered by the reach of her message, she also found herself absorbing a constant stream of hostility—threats, mockery, and character attacks. This exposure gradually eroded her emotional resilience. She began having difficulty sleeping, ruminating on negative comments, and questioning the efficacy of her advocacy.

Zara's turning point came after a digital harassment episode that left her deeply shaken. With the guidance of a youth media literacy programme, she began to develop strategies for emotional boundaries. She learned to delegate moderation responsibilities to trusted allies, created scheduled breaks from posting, and practised what she described as "emotional firewalling"—recognising that not every comment deserved her energy. Importantly, she did not disengage from digital activism. Instead, she diversified her expression, moving some of her work into community zines, in-person workshops, and podcast conversations. Her journey illustrates a mature understanding of *sustainable engagement*—an awareness that visibility should not come at the expense of psychological safety.

These case studies reveal several recurring themes. First, the struggle to maintain emotional equilibrium in the face of constant social feedback is widespread but often under-discussed. Many children internalise digital stress as a personal failing rather than a systemic pressure. Second, the resolution of these struggles is rarely achieved through punitive restrictions. Instead, meaningful change occurs when children are empowered with insight, agency, and alternatives. Whether through reflective journaling, guided counselling, or exposure to healthier online communities, these young people developed the capacity to assess and adjust their digital habits.

One particularly compelling example comes from a middle school in Melbourne, which piloted a "Digital Balance Project" involving students who had experienced online stress. Participants were asked to create "digital autobiographies," chronicling their relationship with technology from their earliest memories to the present. Through writing, drawing, and discussion, students articulated the emotional highs and lows of their screen-based experiences. The process proved revelatory. One student wrote, "I realised I scroll most when I feel bad, but it never makes me feel better." Another reflected, "Posting selfies made me feel powerful until I started waiting for likes." These insights led many to adopt new habits—not from fear, but from clarity.

What binds these stories together is not a rejection of digital culture, but a *reclamation* of personal agency within it. The children and adolescents who successfully rebalanced their online lives did so not by retreating from the digital world, but by learning to inhabit it more consciously. They questioned its scripts, observed its effects on their emotions, and sought out spaces that affirmed rather than fragmented their sense of self. Their experiences underscore a profound truth: that resilience in the digital age is not about disconnection, but about *discernment*.

Parents, educators, and mental health professionals can draw key lessons from these narratives. First, the path to digital well-being is deeply individual. Strategies that work for one child may not work for another. What matters is creating the conditions in which self-awareness can emerge—through dialogue, reflection, and non-judgemental support. Second, young people do not lack the capacity for critical engagement with social media; they often lack the *language* and *space* to articulate it. When those are provided, they demonstrate remarkable insight and adaptability.

Finally, these stories offer hope. In a discourse often dominated by fear—of addiction, comparison, exposure—it is essential to recognise the capacity of young people to self-correct, to seek balance, and to grow. They are not passive victims of digital culture, nor are they naive users. They are participants in a complex ecosystem, capable of navigating it with thoughtfulness and care—so long as we give them the tools, the trust, and the time to do so.

Chapter 6
When Technology Becomes a Problem – Recognising Digital Dependency

In today's families, technology doesn't simply sit in the background—it steps in as a kind of digital cohabitant. It nudges us awake in the mornings, orchestrates the logistics of our day, fills silences with sound and motion, and threads its way through conversations both near and far. For children, its role is even more layered. It is the classroom, the hangout, the hobby corner, and, at times, the emotional escape hatch. Used with care, digital tools can educate, connect, and ignite creativity. But there's a quieter shift that happens when screen use slips from intentional to automatic—from engaged to entranced. That's when it begins to chip away at relationships, sleep, self-regulation. This chapter considers that turning point—when use morphs into dependency—and how families can spot the signs, respond with intention, and gently recalibrate before patterns harden.

Heavy screen use, in itself, isn't the enemy. A teenager spending hours animating, building code, or exchanging thoughts on a history forum is not inherently in trouble. The issue isn't how long, but how deep—and at what cost. Digital dependency announces itself not with a bang, but a slow erosion. You'll see it in the frayed tempers, the missed assignments, the retreat from social circles, the nights stretched thin. It's defined by compulsion in the face of consequence—when the user feels unable to stop, even when the results say they should.

Understanding where immersion ends and compulsion begins isn't easy. It takes more than watching for eye-rolls or tracking screen-time hours. Neuroscience is offering clearer clues. Many digital platforms, especially games and social media, are purpose-built to tap into our brain's reward systems. Dopamine—a chemical central to desire and anticipation—surges in the milliseconds before a like lands, a level loads, or a ping signals approval. Over time, this reward circuitry becomes increasingly sensitive. For adolescents, whose brains are still scaffolding vital regulatory skills, this anticipation-reward cycle can become its own trap. More troubling still, the constant stimulation leaves little room for the quieter, essential skills—patience, boredom tolerance, reflective thinking—that emotional maturity depends on.

A particularly murky area is gaming, especially when microtransactions are involved. What began as optional perks—cosmetic upgrades, new features—has in many titles become something closer to financial bait. Children are drawn in by cleverly engineered mechanics: time-limited deals, flashy "loot boxes," or paywalls disguised as progress. It's not merely about fun anymore; it's about keeping up, staying in, avoiding the imagined shame of falling behind. These systems mimic gambling to a disconcerting degree, prompting countries like Belgium and the Netherlands to draw hard legal lines. Elsewhere, they flourish, slipping easily past the attention of even the most vigilant parents.

Consider a case from Sydney: a twelve-year-old racked up over £1,000 in in-app purchases before anyone noticed. His parents learned of it only when their bank raised a red flag. When asked why he did it, the boy admitted he wasn't even sure—just that "everyone else had it" and the skin would be gone soon. His words echo a manufactured urgency, a fear not of missing out, but of becoming invisible. For many young users, digital spending isn't just financial; it's emotional, social, even existential.

Beyond the economic traps, digital dependence also invades the body, especially through disrupted sleep. The blue light emitted by screens interferes with melatonin production, making it physiologically harder to wind down. But the bigger problem may be behavioural: the compulsion to check one last message, see one more video, respond to just one more comment. Sleep doesn't only start later—it becomes fragmented, shallow, unrefreshing. Over time, this chronic disruption bleeds into everything: mood, memory, attention, immunity. It's the sort of degradation you don't notice until you're already living in it.

And yet, blaming the child with the glued-to-the-screen gaze risks missing the larger picture. Rarely does dependency grow in isolation. It reflects, and is reinforced by, family dynamics. Children are astute observers; they mirror what they see. When adults are forever refreshing inboxes or scrolling through newsfeeds mid-meal, they set the tempo. When households default to parallel digital lives—each face illuminated by its own screen—they teach disconnection as a norm. And when screens are handed over in times of distress or boredom, they communicate, however unintentionally, that feelings are things to be avoided, not understood. What looks like an individual problem is often a collective rhythm gone awry.

This is why addressing digital overuse must be a family-level shift. Not punishment, not abstinence, but a reorientation—what we might call a digital reset. The exercise included later in this chapter invites families to examine not only how they use technology, but why. What roles has it taken on in your home? What have you stopped doing—or feeling—since screens began filling the gaps? This reset isn't a grand declaration, but a practical realignment. It might mean reintroducing analogue joys, creating screen-free zones, or simply talking more openly about how tech makes each of you feel.

Like all resets worth their salt, this one isn't static. It's a practice. Families evolve, habits creep back, routines falter. What matters is the willingness to return to the conversation. Weekly check-ins, small experiments, shared agreements—these aren't magic, but they help restore agency. And that, really, is the point. A home built on co-ownership and communication has a far better chance of cultivating digital resilience than one governed solely by top-down rules.

It also helps to recognise the emotional roles that digital habits have come to play. For some kids, screens are shelter—from stress, loneliness, or feelings they can't name. For others, they are sources of joy, identity, or even competence that might be missing elsewhere. Stripping away screen time without addressing these deeper emotional dependencies can feel punitive, even cruel. But when you acknowledge the why—when you ask what the screen is standing in for—you gain the opportunity to address the need rather than just the behaviour.

This chapter will explore those deeper distinctions: when overuse slides into dependency, how gamified spending creates psychological traps, how sleep is compromised not just by light but by compulsive engagement, and how the wider family atmosphere can either reinforce or soften those trends. Along the way, we'll ground ourselves in evidence, stories, and practical insights—but always return to a foundational truth: that in matters of digital parenting, connection must come before correction. Children respond not to lectures, but to relationship. They don't need stricter controls so much as they need to feel seen, heard, and part of the process.

Technology isn't going anywhere. Nor should it. But our posture towards it matters. By learning to recognise when tech begins to take more than it gives—and responding with intention rather than alarm—we create space for something far more enduring: a digital life that supports, rather than disrupts, the growth of the people who live it.

The Signs of Digital Overuse vs. Addiction – How to Differentiate Between Heavy Tech Use and Problematic Dependency, with Science-Backed Assessment Tools

In a hyper-connected world where screens have become the default setting for communication, entertainment, and learning, it can be difficult—especially for parents—to determine where "normal" technology use ends and problematic dependency begins. Children today often spend significant portions of their day engaged with digital devices, whether for school assignments, video gaming, chatting with friends, or scrolling social media. For many, these platforms offer genuine benefits: creativity, connection, and even comfort. However, when digital behaviours begin to interfere with other aspects of development—academic performance, social interaction, emotional regulation, or physical health—it raises an important question: is this merely overuse, or has it evolved into something more concerning?

The distinction between heavy use and addiction is not about screen time alone. Hours spent online may serve as a red herring if considered in isolation. A child who spends five hours daily creating digital art, participating in coding communities, or engaging in meaningful online friendships may be deeply invested but not necessarily dependent. In contrast, a child who compulsively scrolls through short-form videos for similar durations, neglects homework, avoids offline relationships, and becomes irritable or anxious when disconnected, may be showing early signs of dependency. The difference lies not in quantity, but in *function and impact.*

Psychologists define behavioural addiction as a pattern of compulsive engagement in a rewarding activity that leads to significant impairment or distress. In the context of digital media, this means repeated failure to control screen use despite adverse consequences. This framework echoes diagnostic criteria used for other behavioural addictions such as gambling or compulsive shopping. Key indicators include preoccupation with digital activity, withdrawal-like symptoms when not engaged, increased tolerance (needing more screen time to feel satisfied), and continued use despite knowing it is causing problems.

The science underpinning this phenomenon is rooted in the brain's reward system. Digital platforms are not passive tools; they are designed with persuasive technology that exploits neurobiological responses. Dopaminergic circuits—the same ones involved in drug addiction—are activated by notifications, likes, messages, and in-game rewards. Each digital interaction offers a microdose of pleasure, training the brain to seek out repeated engagement. For children, whose executive function is still developing, the ability to self-regulate in the face of this design sophistication is limited. This neurobiological vulnerability makes early identification and support essential.

Several assessment tools and behavioural models have been developed to help differentiate overuse from addiction. One widely cited instrument is the Internet Gaming Disorder Test (IGDT-10), adapted from the DSM-5 criteria for behavioural addiction. Though primarily targeted at gaming behaviours, its indicators—

such as loss of interest in offline activities, mood modification through gaming, and deception about time spent online—are applicable across digital domains. Similarly, the Problematic Media Use Measure (PMUM) was designed for parents to evaluate screen behaviour in children aged four to eleven, assessing dimensions such as conflict, withdrawal, and preoccupation.

While these tools provide useful frameworks, they should be interpreted with nuance. Context matters. A child who becomes irritable when a gaming session is interrupted may not be addicted; they may simply be frustrated by a disruption during a competitive or immersive experience. The critical questions are: *How often is this occurring? What is the emotional tone surrounding the behaviour? Is the child returning to screens to cope with negative emotions?* The function of the behaviour—whether it serves as a creative outlet or an emotional crutch—is far more telling than the frequency alone.

Take the example of ten-year-old Noah, whose parents were initially concerned about his constant engagement with a popular multiplayer game. He played for several hours each evening, often losing track of time and becoming upset when asked to log off. However, after a careful observation and a conversation facilitated by a counsellor, it became clear that Noah's behaviour was rooted in social anxiety. The game served as a low-stakes environment where he could interact with peers on his own terms, without the pressure of in-person conversation. His usage, while high, was fulfilling a legitimate psychological need.

The intervention, therefore, focused not on restricting screen time, but on broadening Noah's social confidence offline. As his emotional resilience increased, his dependency on the game naturally diminished. This case highlights the importance of *functionally-informed responses* rather than blanket solutions. Understanding *why* a child turns to technology is a prerequisite to guiding them toward healthier patterns.

For some children, though, the signs are more acute. Thirteen-year-old Layla, for instance, began to skip meals, avoid eye contact, and withdraw from once-loved hobbies as her TikTok consumption escalated. She reported difficulty sleeping, persistent FOMO (fear of missing out), and distress when her posts failed to receive engagement. Her case exemplified the phenomenon of *validation dependency*—a form of emotional dysregulation where self-worth becomes tied to online metrics. Here, digital behaviour was not just excessive but *compensatory*, masking deeper insecurities.

Intervention for Layla involved digital detox strategies combined with therapy to address the underlying emotional patterns. Her recovery was gradual but marked by significant improvements in mood and engagement with offline life. It demonstrated that, while digital addiction may resemble substance addiction in its neurological impact, it requires distinct relational and emotional interventions. Children don't just need control; they need *connection*—with adults who understand, validate, and guide rather than shame or panic.

Family dynamics also play a pivotal role. Children living in households where technology is constantly present—phones at the dinner table, televisions always on, work emails checked at bedtime—are more likely to develop problematic screen habits themselves. Modelling is a powerful educator. If parents use screens to self-soothe, multitask to the point of distraction, or prioritise digital over relational attention, children learn that this is not only acceptable but expected. Shifting family tech culture often involves looking inward as much as outward.

One practical method that can aid in this shift is the use of a "tech audit." Families can chart screen use over a week—not just how much, but when, why, and how it affects mood and behaviour. Patterns often emerge: spikes in screen use after arguments, avoidance of sleep through late-night scrolling, or deterioration in focus after prolonged gaming. These insights provide a basis for targeted, empathetic conversations, rather than arbitrary restrictions. They also open the door to co-creating healthy boundaries—screen-free zones, shared tech activities, and meaningful alternatives that nourish attention and connection.

Educators, too, have a role to play. Classrooms are increasingly saturated with technology, and while digital tools offer powerful educational benefits, they must be deployed mindfully.

Encouraging meta-cognition—getting students to reflect on how they use and respond to digital media—builds the kind of self-awareness that fosters autonomy. Integrating modules on digital well-being into health or life skills curricula can give students the language and frameworks to articulate their experience and seek help when needed.

In navigating the spectrum from overuse to addiction, the goal is not digital abstinence but *digital literacy*—the capacity to use technology in ways that align with one's values, support mental health, and enhance rather than diminish life. Children will make mistakes. They will overuse, seek validation, and occasionally get caught in loops of passive consumption. But with attentive support, open dialogue, and evidence-based tools, they can also learn to course-correct, to step back, and to reclaim control.

Recognising the signs of digital overuse is an act of care. Addressing them with compassion, insight, and intentionality is a form of education—one that empowers children not just to survive in a tech-saturated world, but to *thrive* within it.

Gaming, Gambling, and the Psychology of Microtransactions – How Video Game Mechanics Blur the Lines Between Fun and Financial Risk, and What Parents Should Watch For

What was once a simple pastime—plugging in a cartridge, pressing "start," and playing until the screen said "game over"—has evolved into an immersive, monetised ecosystem where the game never truly ends. Modern video games are no longer confined to static narratives or limited playtime; they are dynamic, persistent worlds filled with social interaction, reward-based incentives, and increasingly, commercial pressure. At the centre of this evolution lies a powerful, profit-driven mechanism: the microtransaction.

Microtransactions refer to small, often in-game purchases made with real currency. These might include cosmetic items, gameplay advantages, loot boxes, or access to exclusive content. While seemingly innocuous—a few pounds spent here or there on a new character skin or weapon upgrade—their psychological design and cumulative impact reveal a more complex reality. For children and adolescents, whose impulse control is still under development, these mechanisms can not only encourage excessive spending but also mimic behavioural patterns associated with gambling. The result is an environment where financial risk is embedded in entertainment and where fun begins to converge with compulsion.

The blurred boundary between gaming and gambling has not gone unnoticed by researchers. Numerous studies have highlighted structural similarities between loot boxes—a popular form of microtransaction—and gambling. Both involve spending money in exchange for a chance at a desirable outcome, often determined by hidden odds. In a loot box system, players pay for a randomised reward—perhaps a rare costume, character, or item—without knowing in advance what they will receive. This uncertainty, paired with the intermittent reward schedule, taps directly into the brain's dopaminergic system, reinforcing behaviour through variable reinforcement. The more one engages, the more one anticipates—and the harder it becomes to stop.

A particularly telling study published in *Addictive Behaviors* (Zendle & Cairns, 2018) demonstrated a significant correlation between loot box expenditure and problem gambling severity. The researchers concluded that the psychological experience of opening loot boxes closely resembled that of placing bets or spinning slot machines, especially for younger users. This association is more than theoretical. Real-world examples abound. In the UK, several families have reported children spending hundreds—even thousands—of pounds on in-game purchases, often without fully grasping the financial consequences. One such case involved an eleven-year-old boy who, in pursuit of rare items in a football game, spent over £1,300 using his father's linked credit card. When confronted, he was remorseful—but also confused. "It didn't feel like real money," he said. The game, designed with colourful graphics and euphoric sound effects, had masked the transaction's seriousness.

It is precisely this masking—of money, odds, and consequences—that makes microtransactions so insidious. Many games use virtual currencies that further detach players from the sense of actual spending. Instead of paying £4.99 for a sword, a child might purchase 500 gems for £4.99, then use 400 of those gems to open a treasure chest. The obfuscation is deliberate. It creates a cognitive gap between action and outcome, reducing the likelihood that players, especially children, will consider the financial implications in real time.

Compounding the issue is the use of "limited-time offers" and other persuasive techniques borrowed from behavioural economics. These tactics are engineered to create urgency and scarcity. "Get this exclusive item before it's gone!" or "Only available for the next 12 hours!" Such messaging activates the fear of missing out (FOMO), compelling impulsive purchases. For children, who are particularly susceptible to peer influence and short-term gratification, these techniques are highly effective. The desire to keep up with friends, not be left out, or maintain status within the game can override developing judgement.

Parents often find themselves unaware of these dynamics until a problem emerges—be it unexpected charges, sleep disruption, or changes in behaviour. What makes intervention so challenging is that the line between engagement and exploitation is not always visible. Many games marketed as free-to-play are built on a "freemium" model: the basic game is accessible, but full enjoyment requires repeated purchases. This model, while financially successful for developers, can place children in a constant state of tension—wanting more but needing to pay, seeking success but encountering paywalls, enjoying play but negotiating pressure.

The psychological toll of these environments is becoming clearer. Beyond financial concerns, excessive engagement with reward-based gaming systems can impact mood regulation, attention span, and real-world socialisation. Children who spend large amounts of time pursuing in-game rewards often experience heightened irritability when interrupted, withdrawal symptoms during disconnection, and even reduced motivation for non-digital activities. In extreme cases, especially when microtransactions are linked to competitive advantage, children may report anxiety, guilt, or depressive symptoms after overspending or failing to obtain desired items.

Yet the solution is not to vilify gaming altogether. Games remain a central, often joyful part of many children's lives. They offer problem-solving challenges, community engagement, and creative storytelling. The goal, then, is not prohibition, but *education and discernment.* Parents must understand the mechanics at work—not just the gameplay, but the embedded commercial strategies—and help their children develop the critical awareness to navigate them.

One useful framework for families is to explore the *intent* behind play. Is the child engaging with the game for fun, creativity, and connection? Or are they returning compulsively, driven by the hope of acquiring a new item or catching up with peers? If the game were stripped of its rewards or microtransactions, would the child still play? These questions can open space for reflection—not as accusations, but as invitations to consider how the game fits into broader emotional and behavioural patterns.

Modelling and boundaries are also essential. When children see parents or older siblings setting spending limits, discussing online purchases openly, or taking breaks from screen time, they internalise these behaviours as normal. Conversations around financial literacy—what money represents, how digital platforms monetise attention, and why pausing before purchasing matters—can be powerful even for younger children. Framing these discussions within values ("we prioritise experiences over things" or "we think carefully before we spend") reinforces consistency and ethical clarity.

Regulation may also have a role to play. Countries such as Belgium and the Netherlands have already restricted or banned loot boxes in games, arguing that their mechanics violate gambling laws. In the UK, growing public pressure has led to calls for stricter oversight and age verification on in-game spending. While legal frameworks evolve slowly, cultural awareness is accelerating. Educators, policymakers, and digital rights advocates increasingly acknowledge that children deserve protection from manipulative design, just as they do from other commercial influences.

The path forward requires vigilance, transparency, and collaboration. Game developers must be held accountable for the psychological architecture of their products. Parents must be equipped with the knowledge to make informed choices and guide their children with empathy. Schools can incorporate digital literacy modules that teach students not just how to use technology, but how to understand its impact on their thinking, behaviour, and values.

Ultimately, microtransactions are not inherently harmful. But when designed without ethical safeguards, and when encountered by young minds without adequate support, they can lay the groundwork for habits that are financially risky and emotionally draining. Recognising the subtle ways in which gaming and gambling converge allows us to intervene—not with fear, but with understanding. It enables us to protect what is joyful in gaming while addressing what is exploitative. And it affirms our responsibility not just to raise gamers, but to raise discerning, digitally literate citizens.

Tech-Induced Sleep Disruptions – The Hidden Effects of Blue Light, Late-Night Scrolling, and Screen-Driven Overstimulation on Children's Sleep Cycles

Sleep is the foundational pillar of childhood development—critical not only for physical growth but also for emotional regulation, cognitive performance, and long-term mental health. Yet in today's digital landscape, sleep is often one of the first casualties of unchecked screen use. As screens extend their reach into every corner of children's lives—from education and entertainment to social connection and downtime—the very rhythms that govern rest and recovery are being silently eroded. What once marked a natural winding down of the day is now delayed, disrupted, or replaced altogether by the flicker of a screen and the pull of digital stimulation. The consequence is a generation of children and adolescents who are chronically sleep-deprived, emotionally dysregulated, and increasingly disconnected from their own circadian rhythms.

To understand how this disruption unfolds, we must begin with the biological underpinnings of sleep. The human sleep-wake cycle, or circadian rhythm, is regulated by light exposure, particularly the blue wavelengths found naturally in daylight. These wavelengths suppress melatonin production—the hormone responsible for inducing drowsiness—and signal to the brain that it is time to stay alert. As night falls and natural light diminishes, melatonin levels rise, preparing the body for rest. This elegant system has evolved over millennia. But in the span of just a few decades, artificial lighting—especially the concentrated blue light emitted by screens—has upended this delicate balance.

Research consistently shows that exposure to blue light from phones, tablets, laptops, and televisions in the hour or two before bed can significantly delay melatonin onset. A landmark study by Harvard Medical School found that individuals exposed to blue light before bedtime experienced a 90-minute delay in melatonin production compared to those reading printed material under dim lighting. For children, whose circadian systems are even more sensitive than adults', the effects are often amplified. Their melatonin suppression is not only more pronounced but also more prolonged, leading to later sleep onset, reduced total sleep time, and compromised sleep quality.

However, it is not merely *light* that disrupts rest—it is *content.* The nature of digital engagement matters. Passive activities like watching a calm, age-appropriate film may have a less stimulating effect than interactive ones such as gaming, social media use, or endless scrolling through short-form videos. These interactive behaviours not only stimulate the brain cognitively but also emotionally. A competitive game, an emotionally charged message, or a provocative video can trigger adrenaline and cortisol—the stress hormones that prepare the body for action, not sleep.

Consider the case of eleven-year-old Amir, whose parents noticed increasing irritability and difficulty concentrating during school mornings. Despite going to bed at a seemingly appropriate time, he appeared tired and unfocused. Upon closer examination, it became evident that Amir was spending up to an hour scrolling through video-sharing platforms after his parents thought he had gone to sleep. The content was light-hearted, but the constant novelty and unpredictability kept his brain alert and craving more. "It helps me relax," he told a school counsellor. In truth, it was doing the opposite—delaying the onset of deep sleep and fragmenting his rest.

Amir's story is far from unique. A survey by Common Sense Media found that 68% of teens bring their phones to bed, with nearly 29% reporting that they sleep with their phones under their pillows. Among pre-teens, similar patterns are emerging, especially in households where devices double as alarm clocks or are used for soothing bedtime routines. While the intent may be innocent—watching a video to wind down or using a calming app—the result is often the opposite: sleep is lightened, fragmented, and delayed, leading to a cascade of daytime difficulties.

Sleep deprivation in children does not always present as drowsiness. Instead, it often manifests as hyperactivity, mood swings, poor impulse control, and academic underperformance. Chronic sleep loss has been linked to increased rates of anxiety and depression in adolescents, impaired executive function, and even long-term cardiovascular risk. In a developing brain, where neural pruning and memory consolidation occur largely during deep sleep, these disruptions carry long-lasting implications.

What makes this issue particularly insidious is that it often goes unrecognised. Parents may interpret irritability as defiance, inattentiveness as laziness, or emotional volatility as "just a phase"—without connecting these symptoms to sleep hygiene. The presence of screens in the bedroom adds to the challenge. A study from the University of California found that children with access to screens in their sleeping areas slept an average of 30 minutes less per night than those without. The difference, while seemingly small, adds up to a significant cumulative sleep debt over time.

Addressing tech-induced sleep disruption begins with awareness—not just of the *quantity* of screen time, but of its *timing*, *content*, and *context*. It involves asking nuanced questions: What does the child do in the final hour before bed? Is the screen passive or interactive? Is the content emotionally neutral or arousing? Is the screen use solitary or social, energising or soothing? These distinctions matter because they inform personalised, sustainable changes rather than blanket restrictions.

Families who make even modest adjustments often see immediate improvements. Creating a 30–60-minute buffer between screen time and bedtime allows melatonin levels to rise naturally. Replacing screens with analogue wind-down routines—reading, journalling, stretching, or quiet conversation—helps cue the body and mind for rest. Where screen use is necessary, such as for digital books or meditation apps, using night-mode settings and blue-light filters can mitigate some of the biological impact. Importantly, these changes are most effective when embraced as *family practices* rather than imposed as *child-only rules*.

The design of the home environment also plays a role. Charging devices outside the bedroom, using traditional alarm clocks instead of phone alarms, and creating visually calming sleep spaces can reinforce the primacy of rest. For older children and teens, conversations about the value of sleep—and how digital behaviour affects it—are key. Adolescents respond better to collaborative problem-solving than to top-down mandates. Framing the issue around *function* ("What helps you wake up feeling better?") rather than *control* ("I'm taking your phone away") invites autonomy and reflection.

Schools can support these efforts by integrating sleep education into health curricula. Helping students understand the neuroscience of rest, the cost of sleep deprivation, and the role of technology in disrupting sleep patterns fosters a culture of awareness and self-regulation. Mental health professionals, too, can incorporate sleep assessments into evaluations of mood, attention, and academic issues—recognising that digital habits and sleep quality are often intimately linked.

What this discussion reveals is that sleep disruption is not simply a by-product of modern life—it is a design failure of our digital ecosystems, compounded by a cultural undervaluing of rest. Children do not choose overstimulation; they adapt to the environments created for them. When those environments are saturated with digital stimuli—constant notifications, algorithmically driven content, and 24/7 accessibility—rest becomes a radical act. Our responsibility is to protect that act, not as a nostalgic return to simpler times, but as a conscious investment in our children's health and potential.

Technology is not inherently the enemy of sleep, but its unchecked presence in bedtime routines is a formidable obstacle. When we understand the biological, behavioural, and emotional dynamics at play, we are better positioned to intervene—gently, thoughtfully, and effectively. By reclaiming the night for rest rather than scrolling, we offer our children more than sleep. We offer them the capacity to learn, to regulate, and to flourish. And that begins, quite literally, with turning the lights down—on the screens, and in the mind.

The Role of Family Dynamics in Tech Dependence – Why Digital Issues Often Reflect Broader Family Habits, and How Parents Can Model Healthy Tech Behaviour

The growing concern over children's dependence on technology often zeroes in on screen time, app addiction, or gaming compulsions. But behind many digital struggles lies a more complex and revealing truth: children's tech habits frequently mirror those of their families. Far from being isolated digital natives navigating a tech-drenched world on their own, children absorb, emulate, and respond to the patterns of digital behaviour modelled at home. The question is not only *how much* time a child spends on a screen, but *what environment shapes their understanding of that screen's role in daily life.*

Family dynamics—emotional climate, communication styles, routines, and modelling—are critical yet often overlooked factors in shaping children's digital engagement. When a child appears digitally dependent, what we often observe is a symptom of a broader relational or environmental pattern. Rather than asking, "Why is this child so addicted to their phone?" it is often more productive to ask, "What is this screen use standing in for?" or "What family practices are reinforcing this dynamic?"

The science behind observational learning makes this clear. Children learn not just through instruction, but through immersion. They watch their caregivers, not only to absorb spoken rules but to interpret *lived values.* If a parent preaches moderation while scrolling through their device during meals, conversations, or playtime, the implicit message is louder than the explicit one. Research from the University of Michigan found that children whose parents are frequently distracted by digital devices—termed "technoference"—are more likely to display attention-seeking behaviours, emotional dysregulation, and increased screen dependence themselves. What this suggests is not causation by content alone, but a disruption of relational presence.

Consider the case of eight-year-old Maya, who struggled with emotional outbursts when asked to stop using her tablet. Her parents, concerned about her growing reliance on screen time, instituted strict time limits. Yet the pattern persisted. Upon closer examination during family therapy, it emerged that both parents used their phones extensively during family downtime—often while relaxing in the same room. The tablet, for Maya, had become a surrogate for connection. When asked what she liked most about playing on it, she replied, "It feels like I'm doing something with someone, even when I'm not." Her statement laid bare a truth that many families inadvertently enact: children often turn to digital spaces to fill emotional gaps created by disconnection in physical ones.

Digital dependence, then, is not always about escape. Sometimes it is about *reaching out.* In households where communication is strained, where stress levels are high, or where availability is limited—whether due to work demands or emotional exhaustion—children often turn to screens not simply because they are engaging, but because they are reliably responsive. Games reward achievement. Social platforms offer recognition. Videos provide predictability. These experiences can feel safer or more validating than inconsistent or distracted attention from family members.

It is also worth considering how household routines shape digital norms. In families without structured boundaries around tech use—no device-free zones, erratic sleep schedules, screens present during meals or commutes—children internalise these patterns as default. The absence of boundaries is not interpreted as freedom; it is interpreted as expectation. In contrast, households that treat technology as a tool rather than a constant companion tend to cultivate more balanced engagement. This does not require draconian rules or idealised unplugged living. It requires *intentionality*. When families articulate shared values about tech use—what it's for, when it belongs, when it doesn't—they create a framework in which children can regulate themselves more effectively.

The emotional tone of digital conversations also matters. When tech use becomes a battleground—an arena of control, punishment, and argument—it often leads to secrecy or rebellion. Children may lie about screen time, use devices in hidden ways, or resist regulation altogether. But when tech is discussed as part of a broader dialogue about well-being—about sleep, focus, relationships, and mental health—it becomes easier for children to connect their behaviour with its effects. Parents who say, "I notice you seem more anxious after a long time on YouTube. Have you noticed that too?" open a reflective door. Those who shout, "Enough already, turn it off!" often slam it shut.

Importantly, parental self-awareness is a cornerstone of any effective intervention. Adults, too, struggle with compulsive checking, late-night scrolling, and the discomfort of disconnection. Naming this honestly, rather than performing perfection, fosters mutual accountability. A parent who says, "I'm trying to stop checking my emails at dinner—it's hard, but I'm working on it," models both vulnerability and growth. It sends the message that self-regulation is not a rule for children, but a practice for everyone. In families where digital reflection becomes a shared endeavour, children are more likely to see it not as punishment, but as self-care.

This modelling extends to emotional regulation. When parents use screens to manage their own stress—numbing with news, retreating into games, or zoning out with streaming—they inadvertently teach that discomfort must be avoided rather than tolerated. Children learn that when things are hard, the answer is escape. In contrast, when parents are willing to sit with frustration, boredom, or conflict without defaulting to screens, they teach that emotional resilience is possible—and preferable.

The socioeconomic context must also be acknowledged. For some families, especially those navigating economic insecurity, long work hours, or limited access to outdoor spaces and extracurricular activities, screens serve as an essential coping tool. In such contexts, blaming parents or pathologising screen time misses the structural realities they face. Instead, the focus should be on support—providing resources, education, and community frameworks that enable healthier tech use without moralising or judgement.

Schools and community organisations can contribute meaningfully here. Family workshops on digital literacy, parent-child co-use events, and accessible guides to healthy tech habits provide concrete tools. But these must be accompanied by a cultural shift—one that moves away from individual blame and toward systemic understanding. Digital dependence is not a character flaw in a child or a failure in a parent. It is a relational signal. One that invites us to examine not just what children are doing online, but what families are doing *together*—and apart—offline.

In the end, technology itself is neutral. It is the *context of its use*—the emotional, relational, and environmental dynamics—that determines whether it enhances or erodes well-being. By looking beyond behaviour to the systems that sustain it, we can move from correction to connection. And by modelling the very balance we hope to instil, parents become not just rule-setters, but co-regulators—guides in a digital landscape that, while ever-changing, remains rooted in the same human needs: attention, presence, and belonging.

Interactive Exercise: A Digital Reset Plan for Families – A Step-by-Step Guide to Recalibrating Tech Habits with Sustainable, Realistic Changes

Resetting a family's relationship with technology is not about enforcing a one-time digital detox or issuing blanket restrictions. It is about building a shared framework of intentionality—an ongoing recalibration that balances the practical realities of modern life with the psychological need for presence, rest, and connection. In many homes, the desire to improve screen habits is present, but the approach is either reactionary or unsustainable. Parents may impose sudden bans after a conflict, only to relax them days later. Children may promise moderation but return to old patterns without guidance or support. This exercise provides a structured, collaborative, and reflective method for recalibrating digital life—one that prioritises autonomy, family cohesion, and realistic behavioural change.

The starting point for any effective reset is self-awareness, and that begins with data. Before setting rules or drawing conclusions, families are encouraged to track their digital behaviour for a full week. This is not merely about counting hours but examining context: when devices are used, why, with what emotional tone, and to what consequence. A twelve-year-old might record that they scroll social media in the morning out of habit, play online games in the afternoon to unwind, and watch videos in bed to fall asleep. A parent might note checking emails during dinner or using their phone to decompress after work. The aim is to observe without judgement. These patterns form the foundation for discussion—not as grounds for discipline, but as shared insights into daily rhythms.

Once patterns have been observed, the next step is to engage in an open, facilitated family conversation. The purpose here is not to critique individual behaviour but to reflect collectively on the broader impact of screen use. Families might ask: What tech habits make us feel more connected? Which ones make us feel more distant? When do we feel most present with each other? What offline activities do we miss—or miss out on—because of screens? These questions move the dialogue from compliance to reflection, allowing each family member to express their experience and values.

The reset process becomes transformative when it shifts from externally imposed regulation to co-created boundaries. Children are far more likely to internalise screen limits when they are invited to help shape them. A family might decide together that devices are not used during meals, that screens go off an hour before bedtime, or that weekends include screen-free outings. The specifics will vary by household, but what matters is the collaborative nature of the agreement. This not only encourages responsibility but also prevents the common pitfall of power struggles that undermine long-term success.

Crucially, the reset must also account for *what fills the space screens leave behind.* Simply removing digital stimuli without offering meaningful alternatives sets the stage for resentment or relapse. Families should explore which offline activities offer a genuine sense of restoration and connection. For some, it may be reading, cooking together, board games, or outdoor play. For others, it might be journalling, arts and crafts, or music. These replacements should not feel punitive or performative; they should be sources of shared joy and identity.

To anchor the reset in daily practice, families can create visual or written agreements—a "Digital Wellbeing Charter" or "Family Tech Pact"—that outline agreed-upon norms. This document is not static. It can be revisited every few weeks to assess what's working, what needs adjustment, and how each person is feeling. The act of reviewing the charter becomes a ritual of accountability and growth, reinforcing that tech boundaries are not about control, but about care.

The reset also benefits from small, symbolic shifts in the home environment. Charging devices outside bedrooms, reintroducing analogue clocks, and creating screen-free zones—such as the dining table or living room—serve as physical cues for new behavioural patterns. These changes help disrupt automatic habits and replace them with moments of intentional presence.

Case studies from real families offer insight into the impact of such a reset. In one household, parents and two teenagers agreed to eliminate screens from all shared meals and to observe a digital sunset—turning off devices at 9:00 PM. After an initial adjustment period, they reported deeper conversations at dinner and improved sleep quality for the teens. In another family, a parent and child agreed to pair daily screen time with an equal period of outdoor activity. This led to the discovery of shared interests in cycling and gardening, reframing the narrative from restriction to enrichment.

Sustainability remains the central challenge. A digital reset is not a one-off solution; it is a mindset. Setbacks will occur—during school holidays, periods of stress, or when routines are disrupted. The key is not perfection but *resilience.* When lapses happen, families can return to the framework, reflect on what changed, and gently recommit. This approach cultivates digital fluency rather than fear, fostering long-term habits of self-regulation.

Parents may also find it helpful to share their own challenges with screen use. When adults admit that they too struggle to disconnect from work emails or mindless scrolling, it models honesty and self-compassion. It also bridges the generational gap in digital experience. Children begin to see their parents not as enforcers, but as fellow navigators of a complex digital world. This mutual understanding deepens trust and reinforces the idea that technology is not a battleground, but a shared responsibility.

Moreover, the reset must be adaptable to developmental stages. A strategy that works for an eight-year-old will differ from one that supports a sixteen-year-old preparing for exams and navigating social identity online. As children grow, so must the family's approach—offering increasing autonomy paired with reflective scaffolding. Teenagers, in particular, benefit from exploring the *why* of digital habits. They are capable of critical thought and often appreciate discussions that treat them as participants in shaping their own lives.

Finally, the broader cultural context must be acknowledged. Screens are not just a family issue; they are woven into the fabric of education, socialisation, and even self-concept. Thus, a digital reset is a form of cultural resistance—not in a reactionary sense, but as a conscious refusal to be passively shaped by design algorithms, advertising pressure, and attention economies. It affirms that the family remains a vital space of agency, reflection, and reorientation.

By crafting a digital reset plan rooted in awareness, collaboration, and care, families can move beyond fear-based responses to screen use. They can build new patterns that honour both the benefits of technology and the deeper needs of human connection. This is not a return to a pre-digital ideal, but a thoughtful progression toward a healthier coexistence—one screen, one moment, one choice at a time.

Chapter 7
Tech as a Tool for Growth and Creativity

For all the worry that surrounds technology's role in childhood, there's a quieter, less explored narrative that deserves equal attention: when digital tools are approached with intention and guided support, they can become engines of creativity, learning, and meaningful contribution. The prevailing conversation about children and screens tends to lean heavily towards caution—cutting back screen time, curbing exposure, preventing addiction. But this chapter turns that framing on its head. Instead of asking how we might pull children away from their devices, the better question is: how can we invite them into engagement not passively, but with purpose, imagination, and a sense of authorship?

This shift in perspective matters. Today's children aren't just growing up with technology; they are growing up inside a digital ecosystem, one where proficiency with tech is no longer a niche advantage but a basic competency. It shapes how they learn, how they connect, how they imagine their futures. In this light, digital parenting isn't about retreat—it's about preparation. A child learning to code isn't simply adding a job-ready skill to their toolkit. They're also cultivating a kind of mental discipline—one that encourages logical reasoning, creativity under constraint, and a quiet confidence in their ability to solve problems. Likewise, a teen creating climate awareness videos on social media isn't wasting time online—they're storytelling with intent, contributing to a broader cultural dialogue.

But such promise doesn't emerge automatically. It requires a redirection—from consumption to creation. Too much of children's screen time today is worryingly passive: scrolling, streaming, playing games engineered to be addictive rather than enriching. These platforms are built to keep users engaged, yes—but engaged in a loop of shallow rewards and mindless repetition. Creativity, on the other hand, demands a different kind of digital relationship. It calls for tools that invite children to shape, to build, to invent: coding their own games, designing animations, composing digital music, editing films, simulating worlds. These acts stretch the brain in productive ways—engaging imagination, focus, and the drive to see an idea through to completion.

There is no shortage of research to back this up. A study by the Joan Ganz Cooney Center, for example, found clear differences between children who used digital media for creative projects—app building, robotics—and those whose usage skewed more passive. The former group demonstrated stronger problem-solving skills, greater persistence, and a higher sense of ownership over their learning. What stood out wasn't merely what they did, but how they felt about doing it. Agency, it turns out, is the real differentiator.

This same principle is gaining ground in the EdTech space. When done well, educational technology can open learning pathways that are personalised and responsive. Adaptive learning systems that adjust to a child's pace and ability can be transformative, particularly for those who struggle in traditional classrooms. Simulations and interactive environments in subjects like physics, history, or maths allow students to visualise and experiment in ways a textbook never could. But here too, there's a catch. Not all EdTech is equal. Parents and educators must remain discerning: which platforms genuinely deepen understanding—and which simply cloak passive engagement in a veneer of productivity?

Then there's the wider horizon of youth-led innovation—proof, if we needed it, that children can use technology not only to grow but to lead. Across the globe, young people are creating tools to solve real problems in their communities. In India, teenagers have developed an app to track and alert residents about water shortages. In the UK, a twelve-year-old built a reading tool designed for children with dyslexia. These aren't just feel-good stories. They're signs of what's possible when children are equipped not just with devices, but with belief—in themselves, and in the idea that their ideas matter.

Of course, such belief doesn't appear out of nowhere. It's nurtured, often quietly, by adults willing to show up—not as experts, but as partners in the journey. The role of the parent here cannot be overstated. Children don't just need access to software and Wi-Fi;

they need the steady presence of someone who asks questions, who listens, who says yes to the messy process of trial and error. Too often, parents step away from their children's digital lives out of fear, confusion, or disapproval. But when a parent leans in—reviews a game prototype, offers feedback on a podcast draft, brainstorms with their child for a new video series—they send a message far more powerful than any screen-time rule: your ideas matter. Your creativity is worth our time.

This encouragement becomes even more essential as children encounter emerging technologies—AI, robotics, virtual reality. These aren't distant frontiers. They're here, shaping everything from job markets to ethical frameworks. Introducing children to these concepts early—not with fear, but with curiosity—helps prepare them for more than just employment. It fosters a mindset of thoughtful engagement. A child who understands the basics of how an algorithm works is better placed to challenge its biases. A teen who dabbles in machine learning may begin to ask hard, important questions about automation and society. This is where education crosses into philosophy—where learning to code also becomes a lesson in citizenship.

To bring these ideas to life, the chapter will spotlight stories of young people using technology not as a shield from the world, but as a bridge into it. There's Anika, a fourteen-year-old in Nairobi, who began coding during the pandemic using nothing more than free online courses. Eighteen months later, she'd created an app to connect elderly residents with volunteers. Or Max, a neurodiverse teenager in New Zealand, who discovered digital animation as a way to articulate his sensory experience—eventually sharing his short films at a local arts festival. In both cases, technology amplified something deeply human: empathy, imagination, connection.

These stories push us to rethink what it really means to be "tech-savvy." It's not just about how quickly someone can troubleshoot a device or master a software programme. It's also about approach—curious, ethical, generative. It's about seeing the screen not just as a source of content, but as a canvas. Because yes, the same platform that numbs can also wake something up. The same tool that distracts can be redirected toward insight. It depends on what we do with it—and why.

This chapter will offer the tools and perspective parents, educators, and carers need to cultivate this richer engagement. We'll look at the common roadblocks—limited time, fear of failure, the ease of passive media—and explore ways to navigate around them. We'll spotlight resources and approaches that centre on making rather than consuming, on active doing over idle watching.

In the end, reimagining the role of technology in a child's life is not about denying its dangers—it's about reclaiming its possibilities. The point is not to strip away devices, but to imbue them with meaning. Not to shrink access, but to deepen its purpose. Not to shield children from the future, but to prepare them to shape it—thoughtfully, imaginatively, and with a sense of integrity. Because somewhere behind every glowing screen is a young mind capable not only of absorbing the world, but of remaking it.

Beyond Consumption – Encouraging Creation Over Passive Use

The image of a child glued to a screen—thumb flicking, eyes glazed, endlessly scrolling—is now an all-too-familiar snapshot of modern childhood. For many parents, the pervasive concern is not simply *how much* time children spend on devices, but *how* they are spending it. The distinction between passive and active engagement lies at the heart of this concern. Passive use—characterised by the uncritical consumption of content, often dictated by algorithms—can quickly become habitual, numbing, and disengaging. In contrast, creative digital activity cultivates agency, curiosity, and innovation. Shifting children from passive scrolling to purposeful creation is not just a behavioural adjustment—it is a philosophical one, requiring a reorientation of values, environments, and expectations.

The allure of passive use is, in many ways, built into the architecture of digital platforms. Infinite scroll, autoplay, personalised feeds—these features are designed to reduce cognitive friction and extend engagement without asking users to exert effort. For children and adolescents, whose self-regulatory capacities are still maturing, these interfaces are particularly compelling. The platforms are not neutral; they are persuasive by design. As such, passivity is not a character flaw in children but a predictable response to systems that reward inertia.

Yet children are not inherently passive beings. From a developmental perspective, they are wired for exploration, experimentation, and expression. Given the right tools, time, and encouragement, most children naturally gravitate toward making—whether it be building forts, crafting stories, or inventing games. The digital world, far from suppressing this instinct, has the potential to amplify it. But doing so requires intentional scaffolding by adults—an environment that prioritises creation, celebrates effort over perfection, and challenges the pervasive narrative that technology is a source of distraction rather than empowerment.

One starting point is to reframe digital devices not as entertainment consoles but as creative studios. A tablet can be a sketchbook, a camera, a music lab, a publishing platform. A laptop can serve as a space for animation, storytelling, coding, or digital architecture. The difference lies not in the tool, but in how it is introduced, contextualised, and supported. Children need permission—and in many cases, direct invitations—to use technology creatively. "Let's make something together" can be a more transformative prompt than "turn that off."

Take, for example, the story of Leo, a ten-year-old who spent hours each evening watching gameplay videos on YouTube. His parents, concerned about the passivity of this routine, decided not to restrict the activity outright but to engage more deeply with his interests. They asked Leo to describe what he liked about the videos, what strategies he admired, and whether he'd ever thought about making his own. This led to a weekend project: scripting, recording, and editing a short tutorial video. The process required Leo to plan, revise, and communicate clearly—skills he had never associated with screen time. Over time, he began to spend more of his digital hours *producing* content rather than consuming it. What changed was not the platform, but the purpose.

Real-world examples of such transformations abound. In Singapore, a group of primary school students used a basic design platform to create digital comics about kindness and empathy, which were later shared with classmates as part of a school-wide initiative. In the United States, twelve-year-old Ava launched a podcast about sustainability after learning how to record and edit audio from free online tutorials. In the UK, a coding club for girls has helped hundreds of young participants build games that reflect their personal stories and values—offering a rare blend of technical skill and self-expression.

The cognitive and emotional benefits of such activities are significant. Research from the University of Wisconsin–Madison found that children who engage in digital creation report higher levels of intrinsic motivation, self-efficacy, and emotional satisfaction than those who engage primarily in consumption. Creative activity demands decision-making, problem-solving, and resilience—all of which are essential life skills. Moreover, it offers children a sense of authorship: the feeling that they are not just navigating a world created by others, but actively contributing to it.

Parents and educators often express concern that encouraging digital creativity may open the floodgates to increased screen time. This fear is understandable but misplaced. The issue is not screen time per se, but screen *quality*. A child who spends two hours building a virtual world, editing a documentary, or composing music is using screens in fundamentally different ways than a child watching algorithmically generated videos. The former involves sustained attention, learning, and output; the latter, passive consumption and fragmented focus. It is not the *duration* that matters most, but the *depth and direction* of engagement.

Supporting this shift also requires adults to move beyond the binary of tech as either harmful or helpful. A child designing a stop-motion film using a tablet is not wasting time simply because a device is involved. Nor is creativity always loud or visibly productive. Sometimes it involves staring at a blank screen, experimenting with code, or rewriting a story draft—activities that look inactive from the outside but reflect deep internal processing.

Valuing these processes means resisting the urge to judge digital engagement by external markers alone.

There are, however, structural barriers to this shift. Many households face limitations in access to high-quality creative software, stable internet, or adult guidance. Schools, too, may prioritise passive digital instruction—such as digital worksheets—over exploratory learning. Overcoming these challenges requires systemic support: access to creative platforms through public libraries or schools, training for parents and educators in digital literacy, and policy frameworks that promote equitable opportunities for digital expression.

Equally important is the cultural narrative surrounding success. Much of children's online experience is shaped by influencers and streamers whose value is measured in views, likes, and monetisation. This can discourage experimentation, particularly when children fear their creations will not be "good enough" to share. Adults must help reorient attention away from external validation and toward the intrinsic joy of making. Celebrating effort, improvement, and originality—rather than polish and popularity—fosters a healthier creative ecosystem.

One approach that has proven effective in both classrooms and homes is to establish dedicated "make time"—structured periods for digital creativity, free from judgement or comparison. During these sessions, children are encouraged to explore without the pressure of producing something shareable. This reintroduces playfulness, a quality often lost when creativity is tied too closely to performance metrics. Over time, children develop not only creative confidence but also the ability to reflect on and refine their work—a capacity that supports academic and emotional growth far beyond the screen.

Ultimately, encouraging creative digital activity is about agency. It is about giving children the tools, the space, and the trust to shape their digital lives with intention. It is also about recognising that the digital world is not separate from the "real" world—it is an extension of it. When children use technology to tell stories, solve problems, or express ideas, they are not escaping reality. They are participating in it, extending their influence into a medium that will shape the future they inherit.

In a media environment saturated with passivity, raising creators is an act of resistance. It affirms that children are not mere consumers of content, but carriers of imagination, capable of shaping their own narratives. And it reminds us that while the digital world may often seem overwhelming, it is also filled with extraordinary potential—for those who are equipped to engage it not with idle thumbs, but with curious minds and creative hearts.

The Potential of EdTech and Interactive Learning – How the Right Apps and Platforms Can Enhance Learning Without Fostering Dependence

Education technology, or EdTech, has emerged as one of the most transformative forces in contemporary learning. It offers a wealth of possibilities: personalised instruction, immersive simulations, real-time feedback, and access to a universe of content beyond the constraints of traditional classrooms. Yet as digital platforms become increasingly central to children's educational experiences, they also raise critical questions. Chief among them is this: how can we harness the benefits of EdTech without cultivating digital dependence or eroding the deeper human elements of learning?

At its best, EdTech is not merely a substitute for traditional instruction—it is an enhancer. It can amplify engagement, deepen conceptual understanding, and provide learners with tailored support that responds to their pace, preferences, and needs. But when misapplied, or when design prioritises screen time over cognitive engagement, it risks turning learning into a shallow, gamified routine—fostering compliance rather than curiosity. The distinction lies not in whether technology is used, but in *how* and *why* it is used. Quality, context, and intentionality matter far more than novelty or volume.

One of the most compelling contributions of EdTech is its capacity for *personalisation.* Unlike the one-size-fits-all model of many traditional classrooms, adaptive learning platforms can adjust content difficulty in real time, based on a student's performance. This allows learners to progress at their own pace, revisit concepts they struggle with, and accelerate through material they've already mastered. Platforms like Khan Academy, DreamBox, and CENTURY Tech use algorithms to guide this process, offering just-in-time scaffolding that supports mastery rather than rote completion. For students who fall behind or who learn in non-linear ways, this adaptability can be liberating.

However, there is a subtle but significant caveat. Personalisation should never become isolation. While algorithms can guide content delivery, they cannot replace the relational aspects of learning: the moments of confusion that lead to insight, the collaborative discussions that expand perspective, the spontaneous questions that shape critical thinking. Effective EdTech must therefore be integrated into broader learning ecosystems that include mentorship, dialogue, and reflection. In this way, technology becomes a tool for differentiation—not a silo for individual consumption.

Equally transformative is the capacity of interactive platforms to turn abstract concepts into concrete experiences. In subjects such as science, mathematics, and history, immersive simulations and gamified environments offer children opportunities to experiment, observe, and engage in hypothesis-driven learning. A student using PhET Interactive Simulations might explore the laws of motion by manipulating variables in a virtual physics lab. Another using Minecraft: Education Edition might recreate historical landmarks or design sustainable cities, bridging creativity and curriculum. These platforms move beyond passive absorption to active experimentation—an approach that research consistently links with deeper retention and transferable understanding.

A noteworthy case comes from Estonia, a country that has become a global leader in integrating digital learning into public education. There, students use apps like ALPA Kids and 99math not only to practise skills but to engage in problem-solving, collaboration, and creative thinking. Importantly, teachers are trained not just in platform mechanics but in pedagogical integration—how to frame EdTech within broader instructional goals. The emphasis is not on replacing the teacher, but on augmenting their capacity to reach diverse learners. This alignment between tool and intention is the hallmark of effective EdTech.

Yet the question of dependency looms large. Many EdTech platforms are designed with user engagement in mind, often borrowing elements from the attention economy—rewards, streaks, and dopamine-driven feedback loops. While these mechanisms can motivate short-term participation, they also risk cultivating reliance on extrinsic validation. Children may become more focused on earning badges than understanding content, more attuned to levelling up than thinking deeply. This is especially problematic when learning becomes contingent on gamified features, undermining the intrinsic motivation that underpins long-term educational growth.

To counter this, the design of EdTech must evolve towards what educational psychologists call *productive struggle*—the space where learners are challenged, supported, and encouraged to wrestle with complexity. Instead of rewarding rapid answers or superficial metrics, platforms can reward persistence, metacognition, and creativity. Some emerging tools already adopt this model. Platforms like Seesaw and Book Creator enable students to document their learning through portfolios, multimedia storytelling, and self-reflection—prioritising expression and ownership over repetition and speed.

Parents and educators also play a vital role in mediating how EdTech is used. Rather than asking, "Is this app educational?", a more powerful question is, "How does this platform support the kind of learning we value?" When EdTech is introduced as a collaborative experience—co-used by parent and child, discussed in classrooms, or reflected upon in journals—it invites metacognition. Children begin to understand not just *what* they are learning, but *how* they are learning—and why it matters. This cultivates agency, a critical buffer against dependence.

Consider the example of Amelia, a nine-year-old who struggled with reading comprehension. Her school introduced her to an AI-powered platform that adapted text levels and offered visual supports. While her skills improved, what made the greatest difference was how the tool was framed. Her teacher encouraged Amelia to set her own reading goals, reflect on the texts she enjoyed, and share her insights with peers. Over time, Amelia began to view the platform not as a crutch, but as a companion in her reading life. The tech supported her development, but the human scaffolding directed her growth.

EdTech also holds potential in bridging educational inequities—if deployed thoughtfully. In underserved communities, mobile learning apps can provide access to high-quality content where physical resources are scarce. Initiatives like Kolibri and OneCourse have brought offline digital learning to students in remote areas, using low-cost devices and solar-powered systems. Yet accessibility must go beyond hardware. Culturally relevant content, language inclusion, and community involvement are essential to ensuring that EdTech uplifts rather than alienates.

A further frontier is the integration of Artificial Intelligence into educational platforms. AI has the potential to provide granular feedback, identify misconceptions, and personalise instruction with unprecedented precision. However, it also raises concerns about data privacy, algorithmic bias, and the erosion of human judgement in educational decision-making. The ethical implementation of AI in EdTech demands transparency, accountability, and the prioritisation of learner well-being above all else.

Ultimately, the promise of EdTech is not in its capacity to dazzle but in its capacity to *deepen*. It should not replace teachers but empower them. It should not entertain children into compliance but challenge them into curiosity. It should not foster reliance on screens but build bridges to ideas, to communities, and to the self.

To realise this vision, stakeholders across the ecosystem—developers, educators, parents, policymakers—must commit to a shared standard: that EdTech must enhance learning without undermining independence, agency, or critical thought. The question is no longer whether technology belongs in education. It does. The question is: will we use it to amplify the minds of our children, or to automate them?

The answer lies not in the code, but in the choices we make. With careful design, guided use, and a clear vision of education as a human, relational, and intellectually expansive process, EdTech can fulfil its potential—not as a screen to stare at, but as a window to a broader world of learning.

Tech for Good – Raising Digital Changemakers

The prevailing discourse on young people and technology often gravitates toward concern—concern over screen addiction, online safety, and declining attention spans. Yet buried beneath this reactive narrative is a compelling and transformative truth: today's children and teens have unprecedented access to tools that can enable social change, innovation, and global engagement. They are not only passive users of technology but, when given the opportunity and encouragement, powerful agents of digital transformation. Raising digital changemakers means shifting our focus from fear to possibility—from merely regulating use to empowering purpose.

At its core, "tech for good" is not simply about using digital tools for educational or productive purposes. It is about harnessing the creative and connective potential of technology to address real-world problems, build inclusive communities, and foster civic participation. For children and teenagers, this begins with recognising that their voices matter and that the digital platforms they inhabit—whether social media networks, content creation spaces, or coding environments—can be vehicles for agency and activism.

This is not a speculative ideal but an observable phenomenon. Across the globe, young people are using technology to raise awareness, mobilise support, and design solutions to challenges that span environmental sustainability, racial justice, mental health, education inequality, and more. These are not extracurricular activities—they are expressions of a generation fluent in digital communication and eager to contribute meaningfully to the world they are inheriting.

Consider the story of Gitanjali Rao, a teenage scientist and inventor from the United States who, at the age of fifteen, developed an artificial intelligence tool called Kindly to detect and prevent cyberbullying. Using natural language processing, the tool analyses messages in real time and suggests alternatives, encouraging empathy over aggression. Gitanjali's innovation emerged not from a university lab, but from her bedroom and a deep concern about the hostile dynamics she observed online. Her success speaks not just to technical skill but to a mindset: one that sees technology not as a source of harm but as a medium for healing.

Or take the example of Vinisha Umashankar from India, who designed a solar-powered ironing cart to reduce carbon emissions from charcoal-based street vendors. Her innovation earned her a finalist spot at the Earthshot Prize and positioned her as a young voice in global climate advocacy. Importantly, Vinisha's project was not born from theoretical engagement, but from observing her local community, identifying a problem, and applying practical digital design skills to craft a solution. This is the essence of digital changemaking—blending empathy, observation, and action through technological means.

What enables such stories is not innate genius but access, encouragement, and purpose. Children and teens need environments that normalise problem-solving, celebrate experimentation, and cultivate digital literacy not just as a technical skill set but as a civic one. Schools, homes, and community spaces play a critical role in fostering this ethos. When digital learning is framed as a way to "make a difference" rather than simply "get ahead," motivation shifts from extrinsic reward to intrinsic purpose.

The educational implications are profound. Instead of viewing coding, media literacy, or data science as niche subjects, we might frame them as modern literacies essential to democratic participation. Knowing how to code is not merely a career skill—it is a language of creation. Understanding how algorithms shape information access is not just about media studies—it is about intellectual sovereignty. Teaching children to critically assess data, question design ethics, and evaluate online discourse is not supplemental—it is foundational to raising thoughtful, empowered citizens in a digital world.

This can begin at any age. A nine-year-old might use a basic website builder to create a digital magazine advocating for animal rights. A twelve-year-old could use storytelling apps to highlight stories of local frontline workers during a health crisis. A fifteen-year-old might launch a YouTube channel demystifying science topics for younger peers. The tools exist, the ideas are present, and the motivation—when not stifled by fear or overregulation—is often intrinsic. What's required is scaffolding: supportive adults, safe digital spaces, and a culture that values contribution over consumption.

Parents and caregivers have an especially important role to play. Too often, young people's digital worlds are dismissed as trivial or dangerous, especially when adults feel outpaced by technological change. But digital parenting need not require technical mastery. It requires curiosity, presence, and dialogue. Asking a child what they care about, what issues matter to them, and how they might use their favourite apps or platforms to express those concerns can open pathways to deeper engagement. Encouraging them to share their digital creations, reflect on their digital footprints, and evaluate the social impact of their online behaviour helps develop critical thinking and civic orientation.

It is equally important to challenge the narrow definitions of "activism" that dominate public discourse. Not every changemaker leads a protest or writes viral tweets. Some design tools that make everyday life more equitable. Some create art that shifts perception. Some build communities where others feel seen. Technology amplifies all of these contributions, enabling even the quietest children to speak with clarity and reach. A young person who moderates a peer support forum, translates health information into accessible formats, or develops an app for neurodiverse communication is enacting digital changemaking—no less than those on the global stage.

The broader societal context must also be considered. The digital world is rife with misinformation, polarisation, and commercial manipulation. Yet it is also a space where authentic stories rise, marginalised voices find amplification, and decentralised innovation occurs. Raising digital changemakers does not mean shielding children from the internet's flaws, but preparing them to navigate and reshape it. It means helping them ask critical questions: Who designs the platforms I use? Whose stories are missing here? What kind of digital culture do I want to co-create?

Such reflection, paired with action, defines the digital changemaker. It is not a label to be bestowed upon a select few, but a developmental pathway open to many—when nurtured with care, clarity, and courage.

One of the most promising developments in this field is the emergence of global youth networks that support tech-based social innovation. Initiatives like Technovation Girls, GenZ Talks, and UNICEF's Voices of Youth offer structured platforms where children and teens can pitch ideas, access mentors, and collaborate with peers across borders. These communities not only provide resources and visibility but also reinforce a crucial message: you are not alone in wanting to make a difference.

For adults designing these opportunities—educators, developers, policymakers—the priority should be inclusivity. Changemaking should not be the preserve of the well-resourced or the technically gifted. It must be made accessible to young people from diverse backgrounds, with diverse abilities, and with diverse experiences. This means addressing barriers such as device access, language limitations, and cultural representation. It also means designing tools that prioritise co-creation, flexibility, and real-world relevance over gamification and shallow metrics.

At its most powerful, tech for good reframes childhood not as a stage of preparation but as a stage of contribution. It honours the fact that children are not just future citizens—they are present ones, capable of insight, action, and leadership. In a world grappling with complex crises, this recognition is not just empowering—it is essential.

To raise digital changemakers is to raise critical thinkers, compassionate builders, and ethical technologists. It is to believe that a child with a device can be a force for equity, sustainability, and truth. And it is to realise that, amid the noise of the digital age, there is also a signal—a generation ready to use technology not merely to entertain or consume, but to create, to uplift, and to transform.

Coding, Robotics, and AI – Preparing Kids for the Future

In a world increasingly governed by algorithms and automated systems, equipping children with the knowledge to understand, shape, and even challenge these technologies is no longer optional—it is essential. Coding, robotics, and artificial intelligence (AI) are not futuristic curiosities; they are foundational elements of contemporary society. They influence how we work, communicate, learn, and solve global challenges. For today's young generation, digital fluency in these domains will determine not only employability but also civic participation, creative innovation, and ethical discernment in a tech-driven age.

Yet the prospect of introducing children to these fields often intimidates parents. Many feel unequipped by their own educational backgrounds, or worry about pushing children into overly specialised skills too early. The key, however, is not in teaching children to become software engineers overnight, but in cultivating *computational thinking*—a mindset that values logic, problem decomposition, pattern recognition, and algorithmic design. These cognitive tools are transferrable across disciplines and careers, fostering resilience and adaptability in a landscape where job roles are in constant evolution.

The first step in this process is demystifying coding. Often perceived as the domain of adult programmers, coding is increasingly accessible to children through intuitive, playful platforms that require no prior knowledge. Tools like Scratch, developed by the MIT Media Lab, allow children as young as seven to build interactive stories, games, and animations using visual code blocks. These experiences cultivate creativity and sequential reasoning while offering immediate feedback—an ideal entry point for young learners. Importantly, platforms like these emphasise *making*, not memorising—encouraging children to express ideas, test hypotheses, and iterate.

One compelling case is that of thirteen-year-old Zara from Manchester, who began using Scratch during a school project on storytelling. Over time, her interest in narrative design merged with interactive programming, and she created a game based on folklore from her family's heritage. This project not only deepened her coding skills but also became a medium for cultural exploration and digital expression. Such stories highlight how coding, when framed as a tool for storytelling and creativity, becomes far more than a technical exercise—it becomes a form of literacy.

As children grow, they can be introduced to more advanced platforms like Python, Arduino, or JavaScript, depending on their interest and capacity. The goal is not to rush complexity but to sustain curiosity. Platforms like Tynker and Code.org offer structured progressions from beginner to advanced projects, often integrated with real-world themes like climate action, art, or space exploration. These interdisciplinary connections help children see coding not as an isolated skill but as a language that interacts with every facet of life.

Robotics offers another highly engaging entry point, combining tangible, hands-on learning with digital logic. Kits like LEGO Mindstorms, VEX Robotics, or Micro:bit introduce children to the relationship between software and hardware—how instructions translate into movement, reaction, or adaptation. Robotics also introduces key engineering principles and encourages collaboration, as students often work in teams to design and troubleshoot machines that can complete tasks or respond to environmental input.

Schools that have embraced robotics as part of their curriculum often report increased engagement among students who previously showed little interest in traditional STEM subjects. At a primary school in Nairobi, a robotics club designed a low-cost automated irrigation system using recycled materials and open-source microcontrollers. This project merged environmental science with coding and engineering, demonstrating how robotics can foster both local problem-solving and global awareness. It also reinforced the idea that meaningful technological engagement is not limited to elite institutions or wealthy communities—it can be locally grounded and widely accessible.

Artificial intelligence presents a more complex, but increasingly necessary, frontier. AI is now embedded in everything from search engines and recommendation systems to facial recognition and voice assistants. For children, understanding how these systems work—how they learn, make decisions, and reflect biases—is crucial to developing digital agency. This does not mean teaching neural networks to eight-year-olds, but it does mean introducing the concepts of data, patterns, training, and ethical implications in age-appropriate ways.

Several platforms now make AI education accessible to young learners. Google's Teachable Machine, for example, allows students to train simple machine learning models using images, sounds, or poses. The process is visual, interactive, and intuitive, offering a gateway into more sophisticated understanding. More importantly, it prompts questions: Where does the training data come from? What happens when the model makes a mistake? Why does it favour some results over others? These are not just technical inquiries—they are ethical ones.

Helping children engage with these questions lays the groundwork for future responsibility. AI systems are only as fair, accurate, and inclusive as the data and intentions behind them. Teaching children to recognise algorithmic bias, data privacy risks, and the potential for automation to amplify inequality is a form of civic education. It empowers them to shape technology consciously rather than accept it passively.

Parents play a pivotal role in cultivating this mindset. While not all parents will feel confident teaching technical skills, all can foster inquiry. Asking open-ended questions about the apps children use, the games they play, or the content they see online creates a space for critical thinking. Encouraging children to ask "how was this made?" or "what choices did the designer make?" transforms them from consumers into analysts—and eventually, creators.

Equally important is the modelling of a healthy relationship with technology. Parents who are willing to learn alongside their children, to explore new tools, to admit what they don't know, and to experiment openly demonstrate that technological fluency is not about perfection—it's about participation. Children absorb not only what adults teach, but how they approach learning itself.

It is also essential to recognise and support diverse pathways into tech. Coding and robotics should not be framed as purely mathematical or scientific pursuits. They intersect with art, music, language, and social science. A child interested in storytelling may build an interactive narrative game. One fascinated by social justice may design a chatbot to help users understand their legal rights. One drawn to the environment may develop an AI model that tracks pollution patterns. These intersections not only broaden engagement but reflect the multifaceted nature of future careers.

Indeed, the future of work will not be defined by any single skill but by the ability to learn continuously, adapt quickly, and think critically across domains. The World Economic Forum projects that by 2030, over half of the jobs that today's students will hold do not yet exist. What we can predict is that digital fluency, creative problem-solving, and ethical reasoning will be central to nearly all of them. Coding, robotics, and AI are not end goals—they are lenses through which children can understand and shape the world.

We should also remain mindful that not every child will become a developer, engineer, or data scientist—and that is perfectly fine. But every child will live in a world profoundly shaped by these technologies. Whether they pursue medicine, law, education, design, or public service, understanding how machines process information, how systems can be gamed, or how digital tools can be leveraged for social impact will be part of their intellectual and professional toolkit.

Preparing children for this future means cultivating not just technical skills, but confidence, curiosity, and conscience. It means creating environments where failure is normalised, questions are celebrated, and creativity is paramount. It means treating children not as digital natives by default, but as digital citizens by design—capable of shaping the technologies that will, in turn, shape them.

In doing so, we not only future-proof their careers—we empower them to participate fully in the complex, interconnected, and deeply human world ahead. Coding, robotics, and AI are not the future. They are the present. And the children who understand them, question them, and innovate with them will not merely adapt—they will lead.

Case Study: Stories of Kids Using Tech for Positive Impact – Inspiring Examples of Children and Teens Who Turned Digital Engagement into Real-World Success

In a media landscape often dominated by cautionary tales of screen addiction, cyberbullying, and digital distraction, it is both refreshing and essential to amplify a counter-narrative—one that reveals how children and teens are using technology not merely for entertainment, but as a means of transformation. Across continents, disciplines, and platforms, young people are demonstrating how digital fluency, when paired with curiosity, empathy, and purpose, can become a powerful force for positive impact. These are not prodigies in exclusive labs or privileged outliers; they are everyday children reimagining the potential of their digital tools to solve problems, express identity, and foster connection in the real world.

Take the story of Samaira Mehta, a child from California who, at the age of eight, invented *CoderBunnyz*, a board game designed to teach basic programming concepts through play. What began as a personal project—sparked by her own learning struggles with coding—quickly grew into a global teaching tool. Samaira has since conducted over a hundred workshops, reaching more than 15,000 students, and collaborated with Google and Microsoft on digital literacy initiatives. The impact of her work is not simply in the game itself, but in the confidence it has instilled in other children, particularly girls and underrepresented minorities, to see coding not as an intimidating abstraction, but as an accessible and empowering language.

In Kenya, twelve-year-old Clinton Otieno noticed the difficulty many local students faced in accessing educational resources. Motivated by this digital divide, he began using an open-source coding platform to build a basic educational app that aggregated textbooks, study guides, and examination questions into a mobile-friendly format. With minimal formal training and intermittent internet access, Clinton exemplified a kind of grassroots innovation that challenges the notion that technological contribution requires high-end infrastructure. His app, later supported by a Nairobi-based nonprofit, is now used in several schools across his region, illustrating how community-conscious innovation can flourish even under constraints.

These stories are not anomalies. They are the product of an evolving digital environment where children are increasingly exposed to tools that enable creation rather than consumption. The democratisation of app development platforms, low-cost hardware like Raspberry Pi, and open-access learning resources has removed many of the traditional gatekeepers of technological innovation. Yet the catalyst remains the same: intrinsic motivation combined with a sense of responsibility towards others.

In Canada, ten-year-old Maria Keller launched *Read Indeed*, a platform initially designed to distribute donated books through a digital inventory system. As the project grew, she incorporated data analytics to track reading trends, demand hotspots, and distribution efficiency. The platform now functions as a logistical backbone for a literacy campaign that has distributed over 3 million books. What's remarkable is not only the scale of the initiative but the insight that Maria applied digital tools not for novelty but to solve a logistical bottleneck in charitable giving. Her story underscores how digital engagement, when driven by purpose, can enhance rather than displace real-world impact.

A similarly compelling example comes from Bangladesh, where sixteen-year-old Tanzila Rahman used social media platforms to organise digital safety workshops for girls in rural communities. After witnessing her cousin fall victim to online harassment, Tanzila began creating short educational videos in Bangla, covering topics like password security, digital consent, and recognising phishing attempts. Her efforts reached tens of thousands of young people via Facebook and YouTube, prompting local NGOs to collaborate with her in formalising a digital literacy curriculum. Tanzila's approach—combining grassroots outreach with platform-specific communication—reveals how today's teens are not merely digital citizens but *civic technologists*, using the affordances of technology to challenge social norms and foster empowerment.

What these case studies collectively reveal is a shift in the paradigm of digital engagement. While previous generations may have viewed the internet primarily as a repository of information or a space for leisure, today's youth are increasingly using it as a canvas for activism, a toolkit for innovation, and a platform for self-directed learning. The common denominator is not access to elite education or funding but *intentionality*. These children view their digital lives not as separate from their real lives but as deeply interwoven—each click, code, or comment carrying the potential for impact.

This, in turn, has profound implications for how parents, educators, and policymakers approach digital literacy. Rather than focusing exclusively on protection—blocking sites, restricting usage, monitoring time—there is a need to invest in *purposeful engagement*. This means creating environments where children are encouraged to explore meaningful questions: What problem do you care about? How might you use technology to address it? Who else is working on something similar? Such inquiry-based frameworks cultivate both agency and accountability, transforming passive users into intentional contributors.

Real-world educational programmes are beginning to reflect this shift. Initiatives like Technovation Girls challenge participants to develop mobile apps that solve community issues, combining coding with entrepreneurship and storytelling. Similarly, the Global Nomads Group uses virtual exchange platforms to connect students from different cultural backgrounds in digital dialogue projects addressing topics from climate justice to refugee crises.

Participants emerge not only with technical skills but with a broadened worldview and a strengthened sense of empathy—critical attributes for any future leader.

Yet these successes also point to a more uncomfortable truth: opportunities for tech-enabled impact remain unevenly distributed. Socioeconomic barriers, lack of infrastructure, and digital discrimination continue to exclude many children from these pathways. Bridging this divide requires more than device donations. It demands inclusive design, culturally relevant content, and systemic investment in broadband access, educator training, and community-led tech education. Equally, we must challenge gendered and racial stereotypes that subtly shape who is seen—and who sees themselves—as a "tech innovator."

Parents can play a pivotal role in nurturing this potential by validating their children's digital projects as legitimate pursuits. A parent who expresses interest in a child's coding project, helps them research tools, or celebrates the launch of a small app or blog signals that these efforts matter. This validation boosts not only self-confidence but the child's sense that their digital work is not ephemeral, but consequential. Moreover, when adults share their own uncertainties, ask questions, and learn alongside their children, they model a culture of lifelong learning essential to the technological world our children will inherit.

What distinguishes the most impactful digital engagement is not scale, virality, or polish, but *authenticity*. A teenager who moderates an online mental health support group, a ten-year-old who teaches basic coding to peers at a local library, a twelve-year-old who designs an accessibility app for a visually impaired sibling—these efforts, though modest in visibility, represent profound acts of innovation and care. They are proof that digital spaces, when navigated with thoughtfulness and supported by community, can become crucibles of character development.

As we look ahead, the challenge is not to produce more coders or content creators for its own sake. It is to raise children who are curious, conscientious, and creatively engaged with the world around them—online and off. The stories in this chapter are not blueprints to be replicated, but signals of what becomes possible when young people are trusted with tools, supported in their questions, and invited to make meaning rather than noise.

Technology, in the hands of children, is neither inherently problematic nor inherently promising. Its direction is shaped by the guidance, expectations, and values of the adults who surround them. When we encourage children not just to use tech but to *build* with it, not just to follow trends but to challenge them, and not just to learn passively but to lead actively, we do more than shape digital habits—we nurture a generation of changemakers poised to leave the world better than they found it.

Chapter 8
A Balanced Approach to Parenting in the Digital Age

Parenting has always been tethered to the shape of its time—moulded by the pressures and possibilities of each passing era. A century ago, it might have meant steering children through the turbulence of industrialisation; more recently, it was the cultural reshaping wrought by globalisation. And now? Now, it is the ceaseless, humming presence of technology—fast, frictionless, and impossible to ignore—that presents perhaps the most confounding challenge to modern parents. This isn't just another factor to manage. For many children, the digital realm is not a separate activity—it's the air they breathe. And for those raising them, it requires a reframing of role: less warden, more guide; less rule-maker, more co-navigator.

For years, the reigning philosophy in digital parenting was, in a word, control. Install the filters. Enforce the limits. Keep the bad stuff out. On the face of it, this made sense—children were seen as vulnerable, and the internet as a vast, unpredictable territory. But there's a problem baked into this approach: it treats digital engagement as something inherently dangerous, best handled with a firm hand and strict surveillance. And though such methods may yield obedience in the short term, they rarely nurture understanding. More often, they fuel secrecy, a brittle kind of compliance that collapses the moment the watchful eye turns away.

What's needed is not a tighter grip, but a different stance altogether. The future of digital parenting lies not in control, but in collaboration. This model doesn't assume that children are helpless in the face of technology—it recognises that they are, in many ways, its native speakers. The invitation, then, is to engage with them: to ask, listen, and shape digital life together. When families discuss which apps feel nourishing versus numbing, when they make decisions jointly about when to disconnect and why—that's when young people begin to develop something more durable than obedience: they develop discernment.

Here, co-created tech agreements prove far more potent than rigid schedules or blanket bans. These are not static rules taped to the fridge door, but living conversations that evolve alongside a child's growth and a family's shifting rhythm. Maybe it's agreed that phones are put away during meals. Maybe game time follows homework—or better yet, is earned through it. Maybe one night a week becomes a screen-free zone for everyone, adults included. What matters most isn't the rules per se, but the shared reasoning behind them. When children feel they've had a say, they're more inclined to take the rules seriously—not out of fear, but because they understand their purpose.

Such groundwork is all the more vital as we drift further into unfamiliar waters. Artificial intelligence, extended reality, biometric feedback—these aren't future hypotheticals. They're already here, woven into classrooms, gaming platforms, and even children's toys. An AI chatbot that helps with French homework, a VR headset that immerses a child in Ancient Rome, a wearable that tracks focus levels during study time—each new tool brings its own questions. Not just "How does it work?" but "What is it doing to us?"

These aren't only technical questions. They are, in the truest sense, ethical. They ask us to pause and reflect: Who is collecting my child's data, and for what gain? How does this app nudge behaviour, and to what end? Are we expanding young minds, or boxing them in? Parents don't need to be tech experts to tackle these queries—they need to be conversation partners. By exploring these matters together, in age-appropriate ways, they help children build a kind of critical muscle—one that doesn't just follow instructions, but interrogates them.

Take, for instance, the story of a family in London whose teenage son had become deeply absorbed in virtual reality gaming. He spent long hours in these alternate spaces, becoming increasingly distant at home. Rather than slam the lid shut, the parents chose a slower route. They asked him about his experience—what drew him in, what gave him joy, and perhaps, what he was retreating from. Over time, they found ways to reconnect his digital interests to the physical world. They co-created a VR project together, negotiated new rhythms, and wove offline engagements into his week. The end result? A child more balanced, a family more bonded. Not by force, but by shared curiosity and respect.

Of course, for collaboration to flourish, parents need support too. Accessible, thoughtful resources are crucial—tools that don't preach, but empower. The Parent's Digital Toolkit, for instance, is one such resource: an assortment of books, conversation guides, and wellness strategies designed not to impose, but to illuminate. They offer pathways into understanding—not just what children are doing online, but why. What needs are they trying to meet? What patterns in the family are being mirrored or magnified? Apps like Screen Time Genie or platforms like Common Sense Media offer concrete starting points, but the deeper work lies in reflection.

And really, much of that work begins with the tone parents set. Is technology always framed as a battleground? Or is it a terrain of exploration and shared learning? Are adults modelling the very behaviours they urge upon their children—deliberate content choices, meaningful downtime, presence at the dinner table? Children notice. They see whether we put our phones away when we talk to them. They observe how we handle our own tech frustrations. They take in not just the words, but the unspoken messages about what matters.

Ultimately, raising a child who can thrive in the digital age is less about delivering the perfect monologue on screen time, and more about fostering three key qualities. First, discernment—the ability to decide what deserves one's attention. Then restraint—the capacity to resist the compulsive pull of endless scrolls and pings. And finally, responsibility—a grounded awareness of how one's actions ripple outwards, even in a world of ones and zeroes.

These aren't qualities that can be taught in a single talk or downloaded from an app. They emerge, slowly, through practice: trial and error, reflection, ongoing dialogue. They flourish in homes where rest is respected, where presence is prized, and where boundaries are seen not as punishment but as protection. Most importantly, they grow in relationships built on mutual trust, where questions are welcome and curiosity is shared.

This chapter delves into what it means to parent not just reactively, but creatively and intentionally. We'll explore how families can shift from rule enforcement to values-based design. We'll look at how they can prepare for the future not with anxiety, but with flexibility and foresight. And we'll examine how technology, when integrated with care, can become a thread that binds rather than unravels family life.

Because in the end, digital parenting isn't a puzzle to solve once and for all. It's a craft to refine, a conversation to continue. It means creating a home where technology is neither exalted nor demonised, but used in ways that reflect the best of what we hope for our children—and for ourselves. In doing so, we raise not just kids who can navigate the digital landscape, but young people who can shape it—ethically, imaginatively, and with a sense of purpose.

Shifting from Control to Collaboration – Why Authoritative Tech Rules Often Fail, and How Co-Creating Digital Guidelines Leads to Better Outcomes

For decades, conventional parenting models have leaned heavily on a framework of control. When confronted with disruptive behaviour, unfamiliar environments, or new cultural influences, the instinctive parental response has often been to impose structure through top-down rules. In many ways, this has been a natural and even necessary approach. Children require guidance. Boundaries provide security. Structure supports development. But when it comes to digital life—a constantly evolving domain marked by individualised use and highly immersive platforms—the traditional command-and-control model is increasingly proving ineffective, even counterproductive.

Authoritative tech rules, while well-intentioned, often fail because they rely on assumptions that no longer hold. Chief among these is the belief that parents can monitor or manage every aspect of their child's digital engagement. In reality, the ubiquity of connected devices, the sophistication of algorithmic design, and the speed at which platforms evolve mean that most children have multiple points of access to the online world—many of them outside parental visibility. Surveillance-based strategies, such as device monitoring software or rigid screen time quotas, might provide a fleeting sense of control, but they rarely build the skills or values that lead to long-term digital responsibility. Worse still, they can erode trust and encourage children to bypass controls rather than internalise principles.

The deeper flaw with authoritarian digital parenting is that it misunderstands the nature of digital culture itself. Online environments are participatory, customisable, and user-driven. Children grow up expecting to be part of the experience, not just recipients of it. In such a context, parenting that mirrors this participatory model—one based on collaboration, conversation, and co-creation—is far more effective. Rather than framing technology as a threat to be managed, this approach sees it as a context in which mutual learning, negotiation, and shared values can be developed.

Collaboration does not mean abandoning boundaries or relinquishing parental responsibility. It means shifting the mode of engagement—from imposing rules to co-designing them. This subtle but powerful change fosters ownership. When children are involved in crafting the rules that govern their digital lives, they are more likely to understand the rationale behind those rules, feel respected in the process, and adhere to them voluntarily.

One compelling example of this dynamic can be seen in the story of a family in Melbourne navigating their daughter's growing interest in TikTok. Initially alarmed by the platform's content and potential risks, the parents considered banning it altogether. But instead of taking unilateral action, they invited their daughter to explain what she liked about the platform. This led to a broader discussion about what content was appropriate, how to handle negative comments, and when usage felt excessive. Together, they agreed on a set of shared expectations: screen breaks, time limits, content discussions, and even occasional co-viewing. Not only did this reduce conflict and enhance mutual understanding, but the daughter also began self-regulating more effectively—pausing on her own when she sensed overuse, and asking for input when unsure about content.

What this example illustrates is that children are not inherently resistant to rules—they are resistant to rules that feel arbitrary, controlling, or disconnected from their lived reality. When parents listen, validate their children's experiences, and involve them in decision-making, they build a foundation of respect that supports self-regulation. This approach also provides a crucial emotional context: children feel seen, not policed. And when mistakes occur, they are more likely to seek support rather than hide behaviour.

Psychological research supports this shift in approach. Studies in developmental psychology, including those by Dr. Laurence Steinberg and Dr. Diana Baumrind, have consistently shown that authoritative parenting—a balance of high warmth and high structure—leads to better outcomes than authoritarian or permissive models. In the digital context, this translates into clear expectations accompanied by dialogue, flexibility, and empathy. It means recognising that children are developing autonomy, and that guidance must evolve into coaching rather than command.

Collaborative tech parenting also models democratic values. It teaches children that rules are not imposed from above but emerge from negotiation, reflection, and shared responsibility. These are essential skills not just for managing devices but for functioning in a complex, interconnected world. When children participate in shaping digital norms within the family, they are practising civic engagement in its most immediate form—learning to balance rights and responsibilities, to express disagreement constructively, and to consider the impact of their actions on others.

The practice of co-creating digital guidelines can take many forms, and need not be elaborate. Some families use written contracts, while others opt for informal, ongoing conversations. The most important elements are consistency, transparency, and mutual respect. Parents might begin by sharing their own challenges—struggles with distraction, information overload, or screen fatigue—thereby modelling vulnerability and openness. This invites children to reflect honestly on their own digital habits, without fear of punishment or shame.

Another effective strategy is to create regular check-in points: weekly or monthly conversations where screen time, app choices, and digital dilemmas can be reviewed together. These check-ins function not as interrogations, but as spaces for collaborative troubleshooting. They reinforce the idea that digital wellbeing is not a static rule to enforce, but a dynamic process to navigate. Children are encouraged to reflect on how their tech use affects their mood, productivity, and relationships—and to make adjustments accordingly.

Importantly, collaboration does not mean equivalence. Parents still hold the responsibility for safeguarding, and there will be times when non-negotiable limits are necessary—particularly with younger children or in high-risk situations. But even then, explaining the rationale behind a decision and revisiting it over time signals respect and fosters resilience. The goal is not control for its own sake, but *guidance towards independence*.

Cultural context matters here as well. In societies that prize individual autonomy, collaborative parenting may come more naturally. In others, where hierarchical family structures are the norm, this approach may feel unfamiliar or even threatening. Yet the principle of developmental appropriateness transcends culture: as children grow, they seek greater agency. Collaborative digital parenting is not about importing Western liberal ideals, but about aligning guidance with developmental needs. It is about recognising that today's children are digital citizens from the outset, and must be equipped not only to follow rules, but to question, shape, and uphold them.

In this respect, co-created guidelines serve a double function. They regulate behaviour, but they also build capacity. Children who participate in these conversations learn to articulate values, consider consequences, and navigate complexity. These are precisely the skills they will need to thrive in a world where the digital and the ethical are increasingly intertwined.

Parents, too, benefit from this model. They gain insight into their children's interests, worries, and thought processes. They are less likely to feel adversarial or reactive, and more likely to feel connected and confident. Collaboration transforms parenting from a battlefield into a shared exploration—one in which both generations are learning, adapting, and growing.

As digital technologies continue to evolve—bringing with them new risks, opportunities, and ethical dilemmas—this collaborative ethos will only grow more vital. The tools our children use today will shape their identity, their relationships, and their worldview. But how they use those tools—and whether they do so with awareness, integrity, and purpose—depends not only on what we teach them, but how we engage them.

Shifting from control to collaboration is not a loss of authority; it is an investment in influence. It is the recognition that the most enduring guideposts are not those we enforce from above, but those we build together—through trust, dialogue, and a shared commitment to navigating the digital world with intelligence and care.

Developing a Family Tech Agreement – A Customisable Contract for Parents and Kids to Establish Shared Screen-Time Values and Expectations

The notion of a "family tech agreement" may, at first glance, seem like an overly formal approach to managing screen time—more boardroom than bedroom, more contract law than parenting. But this impression masks the deeper value of such agreements: they are not about legalistic enforcement, but about building shared understanding. In an age where digital experiences touch nearly every dimension of a child's life—education, entertainment, communication, and even self-expression—the need for clarity, consistency, and collaboration around digital expectations has never been greater. A thoughtfully crafted family tech agreement is not just a behavioural tool—it is a relational one.

Unlike rigid screen-time rules handed down from on high, a co-authored agreement represents an intentional dialogue between parents and children about values, boundaries, and responsibilities in the digital space. Its power lies not in the document itself, but in the process of creating it. That process invites reflection: What role does technology play in our lives? What are our non-negotiables? Where can we be flexible? And how do we support one another in maintaining a balanced, healthy digital environment?

The psychological backdrop to this approach is clear. Research into adolescent development consistently shows that children are more likely to internalise rules and behave responsibly when they feel included in the decision-making process. The act of co-constructing agreements around digital use cultivates ownership, empathy, and ethical reasoning. It transforms technology from a source of tension into a site for growth, autonomy, and shared accountability.

To appreciate the practical benefits of a family tech agreement, consider the alternative: a household where screen-time policies are either absent, arbitrary, or enforced through conflict. In such environments, children may not fully understand the reasoning behind restrictions. This can lead to resentment, rule-breaking, and reactive power struggles that erode trust. On the other hand, when expectations are developed collaboratively, children learn to anticipate consequences, negotiate respectfully, and reflect on their choices. They also see their parents modelling the very behaviours—self-regulation, boundary-setting, and clear communication—that they are being asked to develop.

One illustrative case comes from a family in Bristol, where tensions around device use had reached a breaking point. The parents, both working professionals, found themselves frustrated by their ten-year-old son's persistent requests for gaming time and their teenager's constant attachment to social media. Instead of resorting to ultimatums, they decided to initiate a family "tech summit." Each family member was invited to share their digital habits, what they valued about screen time, and what they found challenging. This laid the foundation for a mutual agreement covering screen-free meals, bedtime device curfews, weekend gaming limits, and even scheduled "tech sabbath" hours. The most powerful shift wasn't just behavioural—it was relational. Their children felt heard, and the parents gained insight into how and why their kids used technology in the first place.

The most effective family tech agreements are those that combine clarity with flexibility. They are anchored in values—such as respect, balance, and responsibility—rather than in arbitrary numbers. While a daily limit on screen time might be useful, it is equally important to consider context: Is the screen being used for schoolwork, creative expression, social connection, or passive consumption? The same device that delivers mindless scrolling can also be a portal for collaborative storytelling, coding, or video editing. Recognising this nuance helps families move beyond simplistic metrics toward a more qualitative evaluation of digital engagement.

An agreement might also include mutual commitments. Children may agree to unplug devices during meals or avoid using social media during homework time. Parents, in turn, might commit to not checking work emails during family activities or to modelling healthy digital downtime. This reciprocity reinforces the idea that everyone is accountable to the same principles, regardless of age or role. It also humanises the process—showing children that even adults grapple with distraction, overuse, and the temptations of constant connectivity.

Importantly, the creation of a tech agreement should not be a one-off event. As children grow and their digital interests evolve, so too should the agreement. A ten-year-old exploring educational apps has different needs and risks than a fifteen-year-old managing group chats, online gaming, and social media presence. Revisiting the agreement periodically—perhaps once a school term or during holiday transitions—offers an opportunity to re-evaluate what's working, what's not, and what might need to change. This iterative process teaches children that self-governance is not about rigid adherence to rules but about ongoing self-assessment and adaptation.

Furthermore, the agreement serves as a foundation for navigating unforeseen challenges. When a child encounters distressing content, experiences cyberbullying, or struggles with excessive screen use, the existence of a shared framework makes it easier to talk about. The agreement functions not only as a behavioural guideline but as a relational contract—one that assumes goodwill, shared values, and mutual concern. Children are more likely to disclose challenges when they feel that their parents are allies, not adversaries.

In today's rapidly shifting digital ecosystem, such agility is vital. New platforms, features, and risks emerge with stunning speed. Parents cannot anticipate every development, but they can prepare their children to engage critically with new technologies. The family tech agreement becomes a living document—a blueprint for digital citizenship that encourages curiosity, caution, and intentionality.

This principle is being implemented in a growing number of schools and communities as well. Digital citizenship curricula increasingly encourage families to take an active role in shaping tech agreements, recognising that home and school must work in tandem to promote healthy digital habits. Initiatives like Australia's eSafety Commissioner Toolkit and Common Sense Media's family contracts offer templates and conversation starters that help demystify the process and make it accessible, even to families with limited technological literacy.

That said, it is essential to tailor the agreement to the unique rhythms, values, and dynamics of each family. A one-size-fits-all model is rarely effective. What works for a rural family with limited connectivity may differ vastly from an urban household surrounded by devices. Cultural norms, sibling configurations, parental work schedules, and neurodiversity are all important variables. This is why customisability is a strength, not a complication. It allows the agreement to reflect the reality of the family's life, not an idealised version of it.

Moreover, the process of developing a family tech agreement fosters a deeper, more enduring outcome: the normalisation of digital dialogue. It signals to children that conversations about technology are welcome, ongoing, and important—not only when there's a problem or a rule has been broken. This creates a culture of openness, where digital dilemmas are not hidden out of fear but surfaced for support.

As children move into adolescence and eventually adulthood, the internalised scaffolding built through these agreements often proves more durable than any software control. They have practised saying no, setting limits, and making digital choices based on values rather than compulsion. In a world that increasingly rewards reactivity, these are radical and vital skills.

Ultimately, a family tech agreement is not about enforcing compliance. It is about co-authoring a digital ethic. It is a practice in mutual respect, a vehicle for teaching discernment, and a symbol of shared responsibility in a world that often blurs the lines between personal choice and algorithmic influence. When families engage in this process together—with clarity, care, and humility—they create not just a safer digital environment, but a more connected, thoughtful, and resilient family culture.

The Future of Parenting in an AI-Driven World – Preparing for the Next Wave of Emerging Technologies, Including Virtual Reality, AI Tutoring, and Brain-Computer Interfaces

Parenting has always been an evolving endeavour, but never has the rate of required adaptation been so rapid, nor the technological shifts so profound. As artificial intelligence increasingly permeates the daily fabric of children's lives—embedding itself in education, communication, recreation, and even cognition—modern parents face an unprecedented task: raising emotionally intelligent, critically aware, and ethically grounded children in a world where human interaction is increasingly shaped, mediated, and sometimes replaced by machines.

The dawn of the AI-driven world is not on the horizon—it is here. Children are already engaging with machine learning in everyday forms: recommendation algorithms guiding their entertainment choices, AI-driven chatbots offering homework help, and voice assistants interpreting questions, commands, and preferences. What lies ahead, however, promises to be even more transformative. AI tutoring systems are becoming more adaptive, capable of recognising learning patterns and emotional states to personalise educational content. Virtual reality is poised to reconfigure how children experience stories, lessons, and even social interactions. Brain-computer interfaces, once the stuff of speculative fiction, are emerging as a tangible, albeit nascent, technology that will reshape the boundary between thought and action.

In this new technological landscape, parenting cannot rely on inherited scripts. It demands a forward-looking sensibility that is both technologically literate and philosophically grounded. This does not mean that parents must become experts in coding or neuroscience, but it does mean they must become fluent in the ethical, cognitive, and emotional implications of living alongside increasingly intelligent systems.

Consider AI tutoring—platforms that claim to offer hyper-personalised, data-rich education. These tools promise to adapt to a child's pace, style, and gaps in understanding. On the surface, they seem like a dream: targeted, efficient, and tireless educators available on demand. Yet beneath this promise lie crucial questions. How are these systems gathering and interpreting data? Do they reinforce existing biases in pedagogy or language? What happens to the human elements of learning—curiosity, empathy, and the capacity to grapple with ambiguity—when education becomes a closed-loop optimisation problem?

Parents will need to guide their children not only in using these tools, but in understanding their limitations. This means teaching children to ask, *Who made this tool? What data does it learn from? What does it not understand about me as a learner?* In this way, critical AI literacy becomes as essential as digital literacy. The goal is not to instil fear of technology, but to cultivate discernment—a mindset that sees AI not as a neutral arbiter of truth, but as a system built by humans, carrying assumptions, values, and potential flaws.

Virtual reality poses a different set of challenges and opportunities. Already, immersive simulations are being used in classrooms to teach history by walking through ancient cities, or biology by exploring the inside of a cell. For children with disabilities, VR can offer unprecedented access to experiences that would otherwise be inaccessible. But VR also alters the boundary between reality and representation in ways that are neurologically and psychologically potent. Prolonged immersion can affect spatial awareness, emotional regulation, and social processing. More subtly, the narratives embedded in VR environments shape perception, memory, and belief—often without the user's conscious awareness.

The parental role here is twofold. First, to establish practical boundaries around VR use, including duration, safety, and age-appropriate content. Second, and more importantly, to cultivate media awareness. This means helping children reflect on their experiences within virtual spaces: *What did that world prioritise? Whose stories were told? How did it make you feel, and why?* As VR becomes more common in entertainment, therapy, and education, children will need the tools to distinguish immersive learning from ideological conditioning, and to carry critical awareness with them into and out of virtual environments.

Perhaps the most ethically complex and philosophically disorienting frontier is that of brain-computer interfaces (BCIs). Although still in their infancy, BCI technologies are advancing quickly, from external neurofeedback headsets to implantable devices that translate neural signals into digital commands. Originally developed for medical purposes—such as helping paralysed individuals regain communication—BCIs are now being explored as tools for enhancing cognitive performance, accelerating learning, or even enabling 'silent' interaction with digital devices.

This evolution forces parents and society at large to grapple with profound questions about identity, autonomy, and the boundaries of the self. If a child can concentrate better with the aid of a neuro-enhancement device, should that be encouraged? If emotional states can be tracked and optimised through real-time neurofeedback, where does the line fall between support and surveillance? These questions are not theoretical. They are rapidly becoming relevant in classrooms, where companies are piloting EEG headbands to monitor student engagement, and in homes where wellness apps purport to offer mental clarity through brainwave regulation.

Parenting in this context requires a kind of anticipatory ethics—a willingness to wrestle with dilemmas before they are fully formed. It also requires cultivating in children a resilient sense of self that is not dependent on external augmentation. This means grounding them in values that transcend technological trends: empathy, reflection, patience, and the capacity to hold discomfort. As BCIs and other augmentation tools promise to make cognition more efficient, parents will need to defend the value of *inefficiency*—of slow thinking, meandering conversations, and unresolved questions. These are not weaknesses to be optimised away, but essential dimensions of what it means to be human.

At the heart of this new parenting paradigm is a shift in posture. No longer can adults position themselves as authoritative gatekeepers who understand the world better than their children. In many cases, children will surpass their parents in digital fluency at a young age. This can either be a source of anxiety or an opportunity for mutual learning. Families that thrive in the AI age will be those that foster intergenerational curiosity—where children teach parents how to use new tools, and parents teach children how to interpret them wisely.

This mutuality is particularly important when confronting the emotional and relational consequences of emerging technology. As AI systems become more capable of simulating companionship—through conversational bots, virtual pets, or even AI "friends"—children may form bonds with entities that appear to understand, comfort, or entertain them. These relationships, while sometimes beneficial, can also blur boundaries between authenticity and simulation. Parents will need to help children navigate these bonds, distinguishing between emotional support and emotional manipulation, between relationship and response mimicry.

In practical terms, this may mean rethinking how we discuss feelings, relationships, and interpersonal needs at home. If a child turns to an AI chatbot for comfort, what unmet needs is that behaviour signalling? Is there emotional availability, active listening, and psychological safety within the family context? Technology often reveals what is missing in human systems. Wise parenting sees this not as a threat, but as a prompt for deeper connection.

The future of parenting in an AI-driven world will not be defined by rules or checklists. It will be shaped by values, conversations, and a capacity for thoughtful adaptation. Parents must become stewards of context—providing the reflective space in which technology can be questioned, explored, and humanised. This means resisting both fatalism and idealism. AI will not ruin our children, nor will it save them. But how they relate to it—whether with passivity or agency, dependence or curiosity—will be shaped profoundly by the narratives and norms they absorb at home.

Ultimately, emerging technologies challenge us to return to first principles: What kind of adults do we hope to raise? What does it mean to flourish in a digital age? And how can we equip our children not only to survive rapid change, but to shape it with wisdom, integrity, and care?

Parenting in this context is no longer about merely preparing children for a job market or shielding them from harm. It is about mentoring them into thoughtful stewardship of a world where artificial intelligence is increasingly woven into the fabric of identity, cognition, and social life. It is a role that calls for vigilance, humility, and a deep commitment to preserving what makes us most human in a world increasingly driven by machines.

Final Thoughts: Raising Independent, Tech-Savvy Thinkers – The Long-Term Goal of Digital Parenting

At the heart of modern digital parenting lies a pivotal aspiration: to raise children who are not merely compliant users of technology, but independent, critically-minded, and ethically grounded digital citizens. This is a shift in both vision and responsibility. The objective is no longer to shield children from screens or to control their online exposure through restrictive means. Instead, it is to cultivate a generation that can navigate the digital world with discernment, integrity, and confidence—able to engage with emerging technologies not as passive consumers but as thoughtful, empowered participants.

This long-term goal requires a deeper kind of guidance, one that reaches far beyond surface-level rules about screen time or app approvals. It calls for sustained conversations about digital ethics, media literacy, emotional regulation, and the invisible forces shaping online experience. It also demands that parents embrace a new kind of humility: a recognition that they are not the final authority on technology, but co-learners navigating an ever-changing landscape alongside their children. The power of digital parenting in the twenty-first century does not lie in certainty, but in openness, adaptability, and values-based leadership.

The notion of raising independent tech-savvy thinkers begins with a foundational principle: children must be taught to think *about* technology, not just *with* it. In an age where algorithms influence everything from social media feeds to educational content, the capacity to step back and ask critical questions—*Who designed this? What is it optimising for? How is it shaping my behaviour or beliefs?*—is as important as any technical skill. This form of meta-cognition is what distinguishes genuine digital literacy from functional proficiency.

Consider the example of media consumption. A teenager scrolling through a video-sharing platform might easily spend hours immersed in curated content that subtly reinforces confirmation bias or idealised lifestyles. Without the tools to analyse what is being shown—and more importantly, *why*—they may absorb messages that distort self-image, values, or worldview. But with parental support and practice in media literacy, that same teenager can learn to deconstruct content critically: noticing patterns, identifying manipulation, and choosing with intentionality rather than compulsion.

These skills must be nurtured incrementally, with sensitivity to age and developmental stage. For younger children, this might involve guided conversations after watching a cartoon or playing a game. What did the characters do? Was it realistic? How did it make you feel? For adolescents, the discussion becomes more nuanced—exploring topics like digital identity, misinformation, online activism, and data privacy. What is crucial at every stage is that the home becomes a place where technology is discussed as part of life, not as a separate or secret sphere.

The families that model this kind of digital dialogue consistently report more open communication, stronger trust, and fewer conflicts over technology use. In one widely studied case in the Netherlands, researchers followed families who practised "active mediation" (engaging in regular discussion about online content and experiences) versus those who relied on restrictive control. The findings were clear: children in the former group developed stronger critical thinking skills, reported less digital anxiety, and were more likely to seek help when encountering problems online. These are precisely the markers of digital independence.

To support this growth, parents must also be willing to relinquish some control. This may sound counterintuitive, especially given legitimate concerns around cyberbullying, inappropriate content, or addictive design. But overprotection can stunt development just as much as overexposure. Children who are never allowed to make mistakes with technology do not learn how to recover from them. They do not develop the resilience to face digital challenges on their own. Independence must be built through incremental risk-taking, scaffolded by trust and accountability.

One practical application of this principle can be found in how families manage screen time. Rather than imposing top-down limits, parents can encourage children to reflect on their own digital rhythms: *When do I feel energised by tech use? When do I feel drained? What helps me unplug?* These reflective practices build self-awareness and promote internal regulation—far more sustainable than parental timers or digital bans.

Equally important is helping children understand their digital footprint. As AI-driven systems increasingly make decisions based on data patterns—whether in targeted advertising, predictive grading, or content recommendations—young people must be equipped to evaluate their own digital traces. What are they sharing? What are they consenting to? Who has access to their information, and how might it be used? These are no longer abstract concerns. They are practical competencies that influence educational opportunities, employment prospects, and even civic participation.

Parents can support this awareness by modelling transparency. Rather than hiding their own digital struggles, they can speak openly about their habits, mistakes, and evolving strategies for balance. A parent who says, "I've noticed I'm checking email too much in the evenings—I'm trying to set a boundary" normalises the idea that digital self-management is ongoing, imperfect, and worthwhile. This kind of modelling builds relational trust and shows children that digital mastery is not about perfection, but about purposeful engagement.

Moreover, digital independence is not merely about *individual* use; it is equally about *social* responsibility. Tech-savvy thinkers must understand their role within broader ecosystems—how their comments, shares, or silence can amplify or mitigate harm. Teaching children to be upstanders online, to challenge harmful norms, or to support peers facing harassment is as critical as teaching them to spot fake news or secure their passwords.

This is where empathy becomes a cornerstone of digital parenting. In a world that increasingly encourages transactional or performative interactions, families must create space for relational depth. That means fostering emotional literacy, encouraging open dialogue, and resisting the culture of immediacy. The best digital thinkers are also reflective listeners, ethical actors, and compassionate contributors.

The long-term goal of digital parenting, then, is not simply behavioural compliance—it is *character formation.* It is about cultivating integrity in online behaviour, resilience in the face of digital setbacks, and clarity of purpose in a world that offers endless distraction. These qualities are not taught in a single conversation or codified in a one-time agreement. They are nurtured through a thousand small interactions—questions asked at the dinner table, debates held over news stories, debriefs after conflicts, and shared experiments in tech-free time.

As artificial intelligence, virtual reality, and biometric technologies continue to reshape the digital terrain, it is tempting to feel overwhelmed. But within this complexity lies opportunity. Parents do not need all the answers. What they need is a posture of engagement—a willingness to ask, listen, adapt, and stay in conversation. When children see their parents not as judges, but as fellow explorers committed to mutual growth, they are far more likely to internalise the values that foster genuine independence.

In raising independent, tech-savvy thinkers, we are not merely preparing children for the next wave of innovation—we are shaping the moral and cognitive capacities that will determine how that innovation is used. We are inviting them to ask not only, "What can I do with this tool?" but "What kind of person do I want to become while using it?"

The digital future is neither inherently liberating nor inherently harmful. It is a mirror, magnifying the best and worst of human intention. Our children will inherit the tools we build—but they will also inherit the questions we teach them to ask. Let those questions be thoughtful, courageous, and kind. Let them lead not toward control, but toward connection. And let the legacy of digital parenting be not the rules we enforced, but the wisdom we passed on.

Certainly. Please hold a moment while I generate the full article according to your precise specifications. It will appear below once complete.

Interactive Resource: The Parent's Digital Toolkit – A Collection of Recommended Books, Tools, and Digital Wellness Programmes for Continued Learning

As digital technologies evolve at an unrelenting pace, so too must the strategies and frameworks we use to parent wisely within their wake. Raising children in a connected world requires more than instinct or traditional parenting wisdom—it demands intentional, informed, and adaptive approaches grounded in current research and supported by reliable resources. The idea of a "Parent's Digital Toolkit" is not a metaphorical convenience; it is a necessity. Just as one would not attempt to build a house with bare hands, neither should one attempt to guide a child's digital development without the proper instruments of understanding, communication, and action.

The digital toolkit is not simply a list of tools. It is a living repository of knowledge and support—comprising books that foster nuanced thinking, apps that encourage mindful tech use, programmes that equip both parents and children with digital literacy skills, and platforms that provide emotional scaffolding in the face of new online challenges. These resources, when thoughtfully curated and consistently used, enable parents to engage in digital parenting not from a place of fear or reaction, but from clarity, collaboration, and confidence.

Among the most valuable tools in the modern parent's arsenal are books—those that bridge theory and practice, offering insight without condescension. Works such as *The Tech-Wise Family* by Andy Crouch and *Screenwise* by Devorah Heitner are more than advice manuals. They ask parents to reflect on the role of technology in shaping family culture, values, and identity. Crouch, for instance, challenges the passive integration of screens into domestic life, urging families to reclaim agency by designing homes and habits that support relational depth and creativity. Heitner's work, grounded in ethnographic research, focuses on raising "digitally empathetic" children by shifting from surveillance to mentorship—helping parents move from simply managing screen time to modelling integrity in digital spaces.

These texts are particularly effective because they do not treat children as problems to be solved, but as thinkers to be nurtured. They prompt questions such as: What does it mean to live well with technology? How can families cultivate a digital ethos rather than enforce arbitrary rules? What does digital maturity look like at different developmental stages? These reflective prompts are essential for parents who wish to evolve beyond reactive strategies and begin cultivating long-term resilience and intentionality.

Beyond the bookshelf, practical tools and applications offer daily support in building digital habits. Apps like *Forest*, which gamifies focused attention by growing a virtual tree when the user refrains from phone use, have been used successfully by families to encourage presence during shared time. Similarly, *Moment* and *Screen Time* provide detailed breakdowns of digital engagement, helping families assess patterns and co-develop strategies for balance. The value of these tools lies not in the surveillance they offer, but in the conversations they spark. A screen usage report becomes an opportunity—not for judgement—but for collaborative recalibration.

For younger children, platforms like *GoNoodle* and *Headspace for Kids* integrate mindfulness, movement, and screen use in ways that encourage bodily awareness and emotional regulation. These apps, unlike many hyperstimulating games designed for dopamine-driven retention, offer an antidote to digital overload. They demonstrate that technology need not be the enemy of well-being—it can, when carefully chosen, become an ally in emotional growth and attentional control.

Equally important are educational programmes that build foundational digital literacy. Organisations such as *Common Sense Media*, *Internet Matters*, and *Be Internet Awesome* by Google offer age-specific curricula and family resources to help children understand privacy, identity, cyberbullying, misinformation, and online ethics. These initiatives move beyond warnings and prohibitions, focusing instead on equipping children with the analytical skills to navigate complexity. For parents, they offer scripts, guides, and structured activities that facilitate meaningful engagement with difficult topics.

What makes these programmes particularly effective is their emphasis on empowerment over fear. For example, *Common Sense Media's* digital citizenship framework includes modules on media balance, digital footprint, and news credibility. Parents using these modules at home often find themselves learning alongside their children—exploring biases in search algorithms, decoding persuasive design, or reflecting on their own screen habits. This kind of co-learning repositions the parent not as a gatekeeper, but as a guide—a model of curiosity and critical thinking.

But a truly robust digital toolkit also includes platforms that support emotional wellness in the digital context. As children spend more time in online environments, their emotional development is increasingly shaped by digital interactions—some supportive, others harmful. Programmes like *Bark* and *Circle* offer AI-supported monitoring of text and social media for signs of distress, bullying, or risky behaviour. While some parents might view these tools as intrusive, when used transparently and in conjunction with open communication, they can serve as early detection systems—signals that prompt conversations rather than punishments.

Moreover, mindfulness platforms tailored to youth—such as *Smiling Mind* or *Calm Schools Initiative*—help children and teens develop emotional regulation skills in digital and non-digital contexts. These resources are particularly valuable in households navigating anxiety, overstimulation, or sleep disruption linked to tech overuse. Rather than relying solely on parental control settings, they empower children to build inner control—arguably the more sustainable path to digital independence.

Real-world case studies illuminate how these tools work in practice. One London family, for instance, used a combination of *Google Family Link* and weekly digital check-ins to support their 13-year-old daughter's growing engagement with social media. They reviewed her weekly screen report together, discussing not only time spent but also emotional reactions to different platforms. When she reported feeling anxious after extended Instagram use, the family collaboratively adjusted app permissions and began integrating mindfulness breaks using *Headspace*. This approach led not only to reduced screen time, but to increased communication, emotional literacy, and a stronger sense of agency in the child.

Another example comes from a school-parent collaboration in Bangalore, where *Be Internet Awesome* modules were introduced across grades 3 to 8. Parents were encouraged to attend evening workshops and use the programme's family guidebook to initiate conversations at home. Teachers reported a measurable improvement in students' understanding of online risks and rights, while parents noted a shift in their role from enforcer to mentor. The initiative worked because it was not about "controlling children's tech use" but about "enabling their critical engagement."

At its core, the Parent's Digital Toolkit is not a product, but a paradigm. It represents a move away from binary thinking—where technology is either embraced uncritically or demonised absolutely—towards a more nuanced, reflective, and relational approach. It acknowledges that parenting in the digital age is not a fixed skill but a dynamic practice, one that must evolve with each new platform, device, or cultural shift.

Parents need support in this evolution—not just from apps and programmes, but from communities of learning and reflection. Digital wellness circles, parent discussion groups, and even moderated online forums can extend the toolkit by creating spaces for shared inquiry. When parents exchange stories—about screen-time battles, algorithmic rabbit holes, or unexpected tech wins—they begin to map the real terrain of digital childhood. This collective wisdom is perhaps the most valuable resource of all.

The Parent's Digital Toolkit, then, is not a shield against technology but a compass within it. It guides parents not towards control, but towards connection; not towards rigid rules, but towards principled reasoning. It equips families to make decisions grounded in curiosity, integrity, and empathy. And above all, it transforms digital parenting from a reactionary task into a deliberate act of cultural and emotional stewardship.

As new technologies continue to emerge—from generative AI to immersive virtual worlds—the need for robust, adaptive, and reflective parenting resources will only grow. The most effective toolkits will not be those that promise instant solutions, but those that invite enduring dialogue, lifelong learning, and a shared commitment to raising thoughtful, resilient, and ethically aware digital citizens.

About the Author

Sofia Albrecht is a child development researcher and digital education consultant with a passion for helping families bridge the gap between technology and healthy upbringing. Having worked with schools, policymakers, and parent communities across Europe and Asia, Sofia specialises in creating frameworks that encourage digital literacy, emotional well-being, and family balance. Her work is dedicated to guiding parents through the fast-changing digital landscape, empowering them with tools to raise confident, curious, and tech-resilient children. Tech-Savvy Parenting reflects her mission: turning confusion into clarity for the 21st-century parent.

www.ingramcontent.com/pod-product-compliance
Lightning Source LLC
Chambersburg PA
CBHW031345230926
51848CB00002B/392
9789371342452